UNLOCK TEEN BRAINPOWER

UNLOCK TEEN BRAINPOWER

20 Keys to Boosting Attention, Memory, and Efficiency

Judy Willis

Rowman & Littlefield
Lanham • Boulder • New York • London

Published by Rowman & Littlefield
A wholly owned subsidary of
The Rowman & Littlefield Publishing Group, Inc.
4501 Forbes Boulevard, Suite 200, Lanham, Maryland 20706
www.rowman.com

6 Tinworth Street, London SE11 5AL

British Library Cataloguing in Publication Information Available

Library of Congress Cataloging-in-Publication Data Available

ISBN: 978-1-4758-5220-2 (cloth : alk. paper)
ISBN: 978-1-4758-5221-9 (electronic)

∞™ The paper used in this publication meets the minimum requirements of
American National Standard for Information Sciences—Permanence of Paper
for Printed Library Materials, ANSI/NISO Z39.48-1992.

To teens now, all teens to come,
and the teenager that remains in us all.

Contents

An Opening Note to Adults

This book may have caught your interest because you feel your teen struggles with focus, organization, making the best choices, motivation, or prioritizing. The fact is that your teen has lots of company: those challenges confront *all* teens today because of the unique world they were born into. Never before in history has the level of demand on teens exceeded their brains' normal neural development.

Children born after 2000 share the burden of a mismatch between the brains they possess during their teen years and the brains they need. The difficulties arise from the underdevelopment of the highest brain-control centers—the executive functions of organization, planning, judgment, emotional self-management, attention focus, and impulse control. Even in normal teens' healthy brains, this expanded demand on their unprepared neural networks can result in attention difficulties, falling behind in school, disorganization, forgetfulness, frequent mood swings, procrastination, high-risk behaviors, and inadequate skills of judgment, planning, and goal-directed behavior.

This problem became evident to me in my practice as a neurologist. I saw increasing numbers of adolescents and teens referred for evaluation because of parental or teacher concerns that neurological abnormalities were the basis for their problems of attention, memory, thinking, information processing, or other executive functions. Thankfully though, their brains were most often completely normal.

I was engaged in these perplexing and disturbing evaluations of teens misdiagnosed with brain abnormalities. Thankfully, breakthroughs in neuroscience research illuminated the actual problem. To meet the efficiency level needed by today's teens, research revealed that it is possible to boost the development of these executive brain-control centers.

Of note, the research revealed that the teen brain is not a junior adult brain. Rather, it is profoundly different from the brain of either a child or an adult. Most significant of these differences is that the prefrontal cortex, where executive functions are controlled, is the last part of the brain to fully wire into the adult level of efficiency. Although this is not pathological, it often results in *mistaken diagnoses* of brain problems and, disturbingly, overprescribed inappropriate medications accompanied by expensive unnecessary brain "treatments."

Although the brain control centers for executive functions do not wire to maturity until the mid-twenties, teens have the pressing need for these brainpowers now. To meet the challenges and opportunities in today's world, they cannot wait the five to ten more years it takes for their brains to reach their adult levels of highest brainpower.

On recognizing this disconnect between the brains teens need and the brains they have, I dedicated my professional skills to guiding parents, teachers, and teens toward strategies designed for unique qualities of the teen brain—strategies to boost the brainpower they need now, strategies essential to meet the cognitive, emotional, and social demands facing them. Using the revelations from neuroscience research about the phenomenon of *neuroplasticity* (the characteristic of brain networks to become stronger when they are used) and the insights I gained in my practice as a neurologist, mother, and teacher of adolescents and teens, I wrote *Unlock Teen Brainpower* to provide methods for all people—educators, grandparents, coaches, and others, as well as parents—wanting to help the teens in their lives build the brainpower they need.

Unlock Teen Brainpower invites teens to reflect on their challenges and goals and provides simple strategies that will boost the development of the executive-function networks they need to take on the challenges and opportunities of their world. Because they will be guided to recognize the immediate and extended benefits resulting from their actions, their brains will put forth effort to build and sustain these powerful executive function skill sets, which include persevering when confronting problems, considering alternative approaches, planning ahead to achieve goals, and evaluating information from the media for validity.

Their more efficient brains will not only support the skills teens need to successfully negotiate today's world but will also continue to strengthen as they apply them to problem solving, planning, and goal-achievement throughout their life. The resulting brain boost will bring them to adulthood with optimal competence, experience, motivation, and wisdom. They will be prepared for success in college and career as creative innovators, uncovering opportunities never before available.

How to Use *Unlock Teen Brainpower*

This book is organized around five doors that teens will unlock to build the brainpower they need or want; these doors are based on executive-function skills. The chapters are designated as keys, and each key starts with a section titled "WIIFY?": What's in it for you? What challenges will it help teens overcome? What efficiencies will it build and what goals will it help them achieve?

Under sections titled "Gray Matter," teens will learn about each key from a neuroscience perspective. Sections titled "Setting the Stage for Success" will prime their brain by accessing positive memories that they've already stored or by turning on their brains' reward-pleasure response. This response heightens the brain's directed efforts and drive by activating its memories of past success.

In the sections titled "Brain Boosters," there are strategies and activities to build skills. Sections titled "Sparking Your

Synapses" guide teens to write down the specific activities or opportunities to which they'll apply their increasing strengths.

"What Boosted Your Brainpower" invites them to reflect on their progress and on which strategies will be most useful going forward. Throughout the book, notepad icons alert them to anything that has to be written down.

What's in It for Your Teen (and for You, Too!)

Unlike other teen self-help books that put more demands on the parent and seem, to the teen, to be just more homework, *Unlock Teen Brainpower* succeeds because self-discovery and awareness of what's in it for teens motivates their desire to do the activities independently.

Building independence is a big part of the development of teens' strong executive functions. The teen brain has a strong inherent drive for independence and derives satisfaction from successful independent achievements. *Unlock Teen Brainpower* puts teens where they crave to be—in the driver's seat rather than as passengers driven by their parents.

They'll enjoy the independence of choosing which goals they seek and which strategies they want to use to get there. Through the guided progress feedback, while building their brain knowledge and skill sets, they'll become self-directed learners, taking the responsibility for both their failures and their successes. They'll see that setbacks are a matter of failing forward, and they'll comfortably go to second or alternative strategies preselected as the new route to their goal.

Guided to recognize the very early small progress steps to a goal, teens will sustain their motivation buoyed by the awareness that all the credit goes to them for their progress and independent achievements. By forging their own paths, they'll develop grit to persevere through inevitable setbacks, errors, and mistakes, and to learn from them. They also develop the blueprint needed to confidently take on future challenges and aspire to their highest dreams.

As your teen becomes a more self-directed learner, you'll notice positive changes. This will be evident as they become less dependent on your prompts and reminders and increasingly take charge of doing assignments and fulfilling their obligations.

Now turn this book over to your teen, and get ready to move beyond the cajoling, coaxing, and disruptions you've been living with—and to enjoy more time together doing things to make these years before they move on so very special.

—Dr. Judy Willis

Introduction

Do These Sound Familiar?

A teen's life is like an obstacle course—unpredictable, unfair, often overwhelming, and getting tougher each year. Here are the frequent complaints and valid concerns. See if you recognize any.

- *I don't have control of my life.*
- *Everyone tells me what to do. When do I get to decide?*
- *I keep obsessing about the low grade on that test. My parents will be mad and nag me even more. It will mess up my whole grade for the semester.*
- *School is so boring, monotonous, and sometimes seems like a waste of time.*
- *I'm so tired all the time, but there is so much more to do that I can't get to bed.*
- *Sometimes I get so stressed out I feel like the butterflies in my stomach have just pounded down a gallon of caffeine.*
- *There are so many demands on my time and expectations from my school, parents, teams, and clubs that I'm always behind and sometimes just want to give up.*
- *Sometimes I feel like I'm "faking it," and soon my teachers will find out I'm really not smart or my friends will see that I'm really not "cool."*

If you recognize any of those feelings and experiences, I'd like to help you overcome the obstacles that seem to keep you from having control of your life.

Getting Started

At this very moment, your brain is going through a growth spurt unlike any you've ever experienced—or ever will. Your unique teen brain gives you a once-in-a-lifetime opportunity to learn at your fastest speed, activate your creativity, increase your intelligence, and channel your powerful drives to explore and innovate.

The reason? During your teen years, your brain networks are actively under construction and highly responsive to your direction. These networks are the control centers for your highest levels of thinking, remembering, reasoning, planning, organizing, evaluating, regulating your emotions, communicating, and creating—a set of processes known as your executive functions. You were not born with these functions, but you *were* born with the potential to develop them.

Let's consider why you're even reading this book. Although *Unlock Teen Brainpower* can help you get the maximum powers into and out of your extraordinary brain, with more successful results and in less time, I'm guessing that you didn't choose it on your own. It's likely that your parents or another adult bought it for you because they want to help you fix what they see as problems—such as your being scattered or disorganized, not planning ahead, or being impulsive and not considering the consequences of your decisions.

If you're like most teens I've known (including my own, and those I taught in school or cared for as patients in my neurology practice), you don't have an abnormality or neurological disability. Sure, some kids do have real medical diagnoses, like attention disorders and learning disabilities, but I'm here to tell you that most of the problems today's teens have are not the result of anything wrong with their brains, attitudes, or intelligence. The problem your generation faces is that the normal teen brain is no longer adequate to meet the demands of the world you were born into.

Since your birth, there have always been personal computers, the Internet, smartphones, social media, and extensive access to complex information from around the world as it happens. No other generation has had to cope with this growing burden of information. More to learn means more schoolwork. Your easy access to amazing Internet websites, games, and social media is exciting, but being wired in can demand your attention 24/7. Resisting the powerful pull of these distractions requires more willpower than typical teen brains have yet developed.

One cool thing from the latest neuroscience research on the teen brain is awareness about how you can meet these excessive demands. Reading this book, you'll learn about tapping into your ability to change your brain (called neuroplasticity) simply by channeling your thoughts, actions, and experiences. The way neuroplasticity works is similar to how exercise builds your muscle bulk. Each time a brain network (such as one holding a memory or controlling a skill) is activated, as with review of the memory or practice of the skill, the stronger and more powerful it becomes.

You'll start along a path that puts you in charge of boosting the brainpower you need to achieve the goals you choose. By doing simple activities and applying easy-to-use strategies, you'll build your executive functions, allowing you to take charge of your life now and to reach your highest potential.

Using *Unlock Teen Brainpower*

This book includes five doors you'll unlock to build the brainpower you need or want; these doors are based on executive function skills.

Each key starts with a section titled "WIIFY?": What's in it for you? What challenges will it help you overcome? What efficiencies will it build and what goals will it help you achieve?

Under "Gray Matter," you'll learn about each key from a neuroscience perspective. Sections titled "Setting the Stage for Success" will boost your brain's directed efforts and drive by recalling past success or by activating its reward-pleasure response.

In the sections titled "Brain Boosters," there are activities to build your skills and strategies. Some of the strategies are ones you'll be able to apply the same day. Others will be useful for things that week, but depending on your schedule and assignments, you may not get the chance to try them the next day. If the strategy you select doesn't work for you, go back and look at the other ones you thought might be useful. Sections titled "Sparking Your Synapses" will guide you to write down the specific activities or opportunities to which you'll apply your increasing strengths. "What Boosted Your Brainpower" invites you to reflect on your progress and on which strategies will be most useful going forward.

A notepad icon will alert you to anything that has to be written down. You can use a separate notebook, your phone or your computer, or whatever you find most helpful—your choice.

On the very important topic of choice . . .

It's Your Choice

You already know how it feels when you can't get what you want. It took neuroscience research until recently to discover that your brainpower drops when your choices are restricted, and is boosted when you have a say in what you do, and how and when you do it. Following those research insights, this book gives you choices, starting with the goals you want to achieve and in what order. You'll also have choices of which activities and strategies you'll use and the pace at which to progress through the book. You'll get the most from the skills and strategies by using them, so don't rush through the chapters. I promise it will be worth it.

I'm excited to be your guide as you build a lifelong toolkit for succeeding, excelling, and embracing the amazing opportunities that await you.

—Dr. Judy Willis

DOOR ONE

FOCUS

In order to learn, remember, and achieve your goals, you need control over what gets your attention. Focus is what helps you get the most out of your required time in class and reading or doing homework, as well as your leisure time—playing sports or games, and being with friends or family. Focused attention includes blocking out distractions, being mindful of where your attention is, and being able to keep your concentration on the task or experience at hand.

Key 1

Discover the Password for Your Attention Gate

You'll build more control over what information passes through your brain's attention filter.

WIIFY?

- Remembering what you are taught in class so that you can do your homework more efficiently, accurately, and in less time
- Knowing the question the teacher asked or the topic of discussion when you are called on in school
- Keeping track of your assignments and what materials you need when and where
- Keeping your mind on what you read for school
- Remembering what is taught so that you don't have to relearn it for tests
- Following all parts of directions
- Being alert to trick questions and finding your mistakes when you check over your answers before handing in a test paper
- Being thought of as focused, considerate, and responsible
- Having more free time to do what you want to do!

Gray Matter

The attention system is one of the most primitive parts of the human brain. This system was passed on to humans from our mammalian predecessors. The design of this system was very helpful to animals in their wild, unpredictable environments. But as you'll see, it's not the best fit for lives in our predictable homes, schools, and workplaces.

Here's how it works. Survival in the wild is definitely well served by an attention system that gives the most focus (pays the most attention) to things that are unexpected, changing, and different from the usual. It makes sense for an antelope in the wild to have an attention system most responsive to a new rustling in the trees, the distant roar of a lion, or the scent of an approaching predator.

But here are we humans, with an attention system wired to pull our brain's focus to things that are new, different, curious, novel, and changed, yet most of our experiences and environments are very predictable.

No wonder it's hard to pay attention to more of the same when your attention system is looking for, and often finding, things that are new, changing, and curious.

Preheating Your Brain's Positive Expectations

To preheat positive expectations, let's start by busting a myth that causes many teens to be given labels and take on blame for negative things. You've no doubt heard the pronouncement, "You're not paying attention." Well, that's never true because the brain is *always* paying attention unless you're unconscious.

Your body has millions of nerve cell endings that receive information from your senses—the sights, sounds, smells, tastes, touches, and movement around you and from within your own body. Your brain can't process the millions of bits of data it receives every second, so it has a gateway, called the *attention filter*, to select what gets in. This filter keeps out all but about 1 percent of the sensory information. But it is always letting in that same quantity of information each second, so by definition, since your attention filter is letting in sensory information constantly, you are always "paying attention."

When you're not attentive to a lesson or textbook, your attention filter has not stopped letting in its 1 percent. What's happening is that the selected sensory information happens not to be the words on the page or the droning voice, but other more interesting or distracting sights, sensations, and thoughts.

Neuroscience reveals the programming of this attention filter—what information it favors for admission. Because the filter is programmed to give first priority to anything that is new, unusual, or unexpected, what gets in may not be what you need to pay attention to at the moment.

So the next time someone says you're not paying attention, you'll know the neuroscience truth. You are in fact paying attention, just not to the information as it's being presented in your class, a conversation, a film, or a book. You'll soon find out more about how to make things needing your attention more attractive to your attention filter, but for now, be reassured that your brain is always paying attention . . . to something.

Brain Booster

Let's boost your attention power by an experience that will give your brain the feeling of what it is like to have moment-by-moment attention clarity. This will increase its motivation to reach the goal of being able to take charge and direct the attention filter to what to let in.

This is a mindfulness exercise to calm your focus into the moment so that you're fully aware of yourself and the things around you, without any judgments or requirements. This exercise will increase your understanding of what focused attention is like, and you'll discover how many bits of sensory data are competing for entry through your attention filter at all times.

1. Set your phone or another timer for three minutes.
2. Sit in a comfortable chair and close your eyes. Breathe deeply and focus on the feel of the air entering your chest and your chest expanding as it fills. When you breathe out, notice how your rib cage sinks lower as air leaves your lungs.
3. If you find your mind wandering so that you stop paying close attention to the movement of air in your chest, don't be concerned. That's normal. For this awareness-boosting experience, simply take a moment to be aware of what distracted your attention before returning to your mindful breathing.
4. When your timer indicates three minutes are up, finish your breath and open your eyes.
5. Think about what you experienced, and make a list of anything that distracted your attention away from focusing on your breath, including your own thoughts.

It's important to realize that your normal brain has to navigate through this abundance of information all the time to select what gets in through its attention filter. Paying attention to things that are not as curious, interesting, or different as the sensory information all around you is not easy or natural. It takes strong executive functions to take control over the programming for distractions in your attention system.

If you found the mindful breathing helped and you feel alert and focused, you can continue to build your attention potential by spending a few minutes each day on this brain booster. After a few minutes of practice daily for a week or two, your brain's neuroplasticity will lay down a memory track for this activity, so you'll be able to activate it when you feel your attention control dropping.

Sparking Your Synapses

After you've tried out this mindful breathing exercise, practice it several times over the next week. Once a day would be great since it takes only a few minutes of daily practice for your brain's neuroplasticity to lay down a memory track that you'll be able to activate without having to think about it when you feel your attention control dropping. Write down the dates on which you'll plan to do a few minutes of practice in the coming week. ▱

What Boosted Your Brainpower?

You can use these questions as guides for your self-evaluation, or choose your own reflection questions. ▱

- What did I do that was the best use of my time?
- What improvement did I first notice?
- What did I try that I'd do again?
- What would I do differently next time?
- What other strategy from this key do I think will boost my brainpower?

You can create a chart like this one to help you in your evaluation.

Date	Strategy I Tried	What I Noticed
Day 1		
Day 2		
Day 3		
Day 4		
Day 5		

Key 2

Taking Charge of Your Attention-Control System

*Discover what pulls your attention off task
so that you can take control and stay on task.*

WIIFY?

- Keeping your attention focus where you want it even when more interesting things are calling to you
- Recognizing and resisting distraction by things that aren't what you need to get into your brain
- Selecting the most important things to attend to so that you'll remember these for tests
- Getting more out of homework and reading and completing them more effectively

Gray Matter

Now that you know more about your brain's attention filter, you'll be able to use strategies that will put you in the driver's seat to recognize what distractions disrupt your focus and how to keep your attention where it needs to be.

13

As you build your attention skills, it's a great time to understand the power of recognizing your progress. When you make yourself aware of how you are progressing toward your goals, your brain is building self-efficacy—your belief in your ability to succeed and reach those goals—and that will further supercharge and speed up your progress toward other goals you choose.

It takes multiple activations of a circuit for your neuroplastic response to construct strong, efficient neural networks that will hold on to the information or skill. Often these activations are more effective when distributed over time. That's why you'll find it most productive when you work at your own best pace and try the strategies you choose several times over several days.

Setting the Stage for Success

Think for a moment about the things that lessen your attention during class; for example, when a teacher is describing a long assignment, when what you're reading is confusing, when a friend is talking to you, when you're thinking about lunch, or when you're worried about being called on.

If you'd like some help recognizing what might be distractions to you, look at this list of very common distractors reported by other teenagers.

- *In class, things I see or hear outside or in the hall distract me. Then I have trouble remembering instructions I need to follow and due dates. I end up scrambling to do the work at the last minute.*
- *I sit near friends in class who distract me by their conversations. Then I can't remember what I'm taught and so I can't do my homework.*
- *In class, when I need to find something in my disorganized backpack or binder, it may take me a long time. After that distraction, I lose track of what is being said.*
- *When my class is near the cafeteria and I smell food cooking, all I can think about is eating.*
- *If my clothes are too tight or I'm wearing dangling earrings, that's where my attention goes, especially if I'm bored.*

- *When someone next to me is wearing too much perfume or lotion, that's all I can focus on.*
- *If I find change in my pocket and I'm not really into the lesson, I can't help trying to figure how much money there is without looking at the coins.*

Now, think about what makes your attention less focused when you're doing homework. Most teens find that there are patterns related to the types of homework, times of day, or relationship to meals or physical activity that repeatedly ambush their attention and result in homework taking more time to finish. Consider your frequent culprits, such as when what you are reading is confusing, you are hungry, the house is noisy, or you get incoming text messages or phone calls.

It's especially helpful in building your awareness about your distractions if you jot down a note when you become aware of your attention wandering in class or during homework. As you plan more meaningful goals, you'll find these lists of attention robbers helpful. They will help you select strategies to try as you take charge of your attention.

Brain Boosters

These strategies will give you the power to take charge of your attention:

- Write the most important class notes using a different color (or homework notes with a different font). The change will reboot your attention focus as you go.
- Fresh air and good light often fade after doing homework for a while. Renew your attention vigor by opening a window, turning on your best lighting, and boosting your computer screen brightness.
- Move it! Get your blood flowing and give your body and brain muscles a fresh surge of oxygen as you flush away cellular wastes.
- When doing homework, set your watch, phone, or timer to remind you each time fifteen minutes passes. Stop and

evaluate whether you've been working efficiently. If not, make an adjustment to keep focused.

- After finishing an assignment, don't put it away. Finish the next assignment, and you'll be able to return to the first with renewed attention. Your brain will be fresher and more alert to errors when you edit or check your answers.
- Keep a healthy snack nearby so that you don't have to trek to the kitchen and see what you can find. Crunching a carrot or celery stick is a new stimulus to perk up your attention filter.
- In class, sit where you'll be able to get in the most intense sensory input from the sounds, sights, and movements that are part of the instruction.

Sparking Your Synapses

You now have two power packs ready to help you take charge of your attention. By choosing the strategies you think will be best for you, you can move toward your goal of keeping your attention focused.

Lots of the word *you* in the previous paragraph. It's intentional. You'll be discovering the neuroscience behind what makes your brain want to put in effort to do things. A big part of it is the brain's inborn programming to try things when it believes there is something it will get that it wants. So, taking ownership of the goals you choose and being in charge of the strategies you want to try will drive your brainpower to get behind your actions.

Take ownership of the strategies you just read about by writing down in your own words a few that you want to try this week. Then add the outcome you'll be moving toward. 📝

What Boosted Your Brainpower?

You can use these questions as guides for your self-evaluation, or choose your own reflection questions. 📝

- What did I do that was the best use of my time?
- What improvement did I first notice?
- What did I try that I'd do again?
- What would I do differently next time?
- What other strategy from this key do I think will boost my brainpower?

You can create a chart like this one to help you in your evaluation.

Date	Strategy I Tried	What I Noticed
Day 1		
Day 2		
Day 3		
Day 4		
Day 5		

Key 3

Playing Games to Build Your Attention and Concentration

*You can have fun and boost
your focus at the same time.*

WIIFY?

- Staying on tasks longer so that you can complete them in one sitting
- Using your time more efficiently and productively
- Concentrating longer and more successfully, even when the information or task is challenging
- Being aware of and remembering more details
- Holding information in your memory longer

Gray Matter

Focusing and concentrating for long periods (for example, on homework or class instruction) can be challenging. Recall that each time brain networks (such as one used to focus attention) are activated, they become more powerful. You can improve your ability to stay on track with activities and games that fire up your neuroplasticity so that you construct stronger circuits for attention, concentration, and distraction-blocking control.

Setting the Stage for Success

Think of a time you built up a skill by practicing it over and over. It might be how your accuracy and coordination built up by practice in kicking a soccer ball or playing an instrument. Recall how difficult it seemed at first to keep up with experienced players or have decent sounds come out of your instrument, and how far you came with repeating the actions. Bring that memory back when you want your brain to boost its buy-in and effort to building mental muscle, like attention focus.

Brain Boosters

Try some of these games and fun activities; they will build your focus and boost your skills of staying on task, using your time efficiently, and resisting distractions. Make a note about the ones you enjoy, and return to them when you have a free moment or are in a place where you can easily do them.

- At a large school event, challenge yourself to look at the people in the bleachers and, one by one, identify individual faces of the people you know. By lingering on each face long enough to take in the information you need to distinguish it from the others, you'll build your attention focus to detail.
- Practice slow observations, like following the vapor trail of a plane, clouds moving, or a moving snail or caterpillar. This builds your ability to sustain your attention on a slow-moving task, such as reading complicated information in a chapter.
- Draw an outline of an object on your desk, but without looking at your paper. Take three minutes to focus on

the object and move your pencil guided only by what you see. This will increase your skills of sustaining undistracted focus.

- Play Mirror Image with a partner. Use the opposite side of your body in response to what your partner does. If he puts his right hand up, you put your left hand up, just as it would appear if you were looking in a mirror. This builds your attention focus to detail because you need to be intent on the movement your partner makes to resist the natural tendency to use the same side he has; for example, to move your right hand when he moves his right hand.

- Play Concentration with a deck of cards. This game builds your ability to sustain attentive focus for longer periods and to keep multiple items in your attention. Your brain networks will be activated because the amount of information you'll need to hold in attention increases as you need to recall more and more of the cards as they are exposed. Then you must remain focused on the location of these cards so that you can retrieve them for a matched pair. You probably remember how to play this game from your childhood, but just in case . . .

> Using all the cards in a fifty-two-card deck, place them face down in a rectangle, such as four rows of thirteen.
> On each turn a player turns over two cards (one at a time). If the two cards match numbers, such as a 2 of hearts and a 2 of spades, the player keeps the pair and goes again.
> If the two cards don't match, they are turned face down again and the other player gets to pick a pair.
> When all the pairs have been found, the player with the most matches wins.

If you want to play yourself, keep track of the time you begin and the time you successfully match all pairs. Try to get more accurate and faster each time. Keep practicing.

Sparking Your Synapses

You'll further preheat your brainpower effort by making some plans now. For either of the first two brain boosters (finding a face in a crowd or practicing a slow observation), think of a time this week when you can give either of those focus-building activities a try. Write down the date and what you'll try. 🖉

Do the same for one or two of the other brain boosters. Just doing the mental planning and writing it down as something you'll do and when you'll do it activates your brain's preparation to carry out that action. Remember, it won't be like the way your brain responds to homework or tasks others require you to do. The difference is that the plans you write are things you choose to do because you understand how they'll help you boost the attention-brainpower goals you want.

What Boosted Your Brainpower?

You can use these questions as guides for your self-evaluation, or choose your own reflection questions. 🖉

- What did I do that was the best use of my time?
- What improvement did I first notice?
- What did I try that I'd do again?
- What would I do differently next time?
- What other strategy from this key do I think will boost my brainpower?

You can create a chart like this one to help you in your evaluation.

Date	Strategy I Tried	What I Noticed
Day 1		
Day 2		
Day 3		
Day 4		
Day 5		

Key 4

Busting Boredom

Choose goals you want, and your motivation
will bust boredom for work you have to do.

WIIFY?

- Getting your brain to want to do what you have to do, even when it's boring
- Keeping your focus on tasks at your most efficient level so that you finish faster . . . and do a better job

Gray Matter

The human brain evolved to focus on one task at a time. This evolution enabled early humans to give full attention to the tasks needed for the all-important goal of surviving. The most important attention cues for them were about immediate needs, such as getting food or avoiding danger. The cues for these needs usually came from sudden changes in their surroundings, such as movement or new sounds.

Your brain still has this survival programming, so it's natural for your attention to be distracted by movement, changing sounds, flashing lights, bright colors, and especially the conversations of friends talking behind you in class.

Although nowadays you don't usually have to hunt your food or avoid predators, you do have goals you want to achieve. With your goals in mind, you'll be better able to plan strategies that will help you reach them. Your attention-focusing skills will grow by setting and establishing a path to the goals you want to achieve.

When your brain wants the "now" option, it's seeking immediate pleasure instead of working toward your goal. A scan of your brain would reveal more activity in your emotional networks. If you choose to postpone immediate pleasure to achieve a goal, your brain activity is greater in the higher prefrontal cortex networks of executive functions, giving you the power to override your "now" emotional reactions.

Setting the Stage for Success

Think about times when you were able to sustain your attention even when the lesson, reading, assignment, or job was boring, demanding, or complicated and there were things that could easily have distracted your focus away from where you needed it to be.

Examples might include the following:

- Assembling or building a piece of furniture, computer system, or model with complex, detailed instructions
- Following the instructions to learn how to use a new computer program
- Planning for a big party or event that required your attention to a number of tasks over weeks, some of which were tedious or demanding

Set the stage for success now by activating positive expectations. Visualize what would be better in your life when you boost

the brainpowers you choose. Write down the ones that come to mind, or select ones from this list to get your brain revved. ☐
   Imagine what it will be like when you can

- achieve the goals you set;
- get right back to doing something after an interruption;
- feel in control instead of falling behind;
- bust procrastination so that you start tasks early enough to finish them on time—and have more time for what you want to do;
- finish homework in less time and more successfully because you won't waste time zoning out;
- put an end to struggles with your parents or teachers about undone assignments; and
- stop the accusations and untrue beliefs that you are lazy, unmotivated, or defiant.

Brain Boosters

Your brain is more likely to engage responsively when it knows how you will benefit from any activity. Setting your own goals increases your brain's desire to achieve them. The more specifically you define your goal and acknowledge its value to you, the more your brain will put in the effort to achieve it.
   It's likely that you have times when it is hard to remain attentive, especially if the task is boring, annoying, or frustrating. Below are some goals many teens have related to keeping their attention focused. Write down the ones that are your attention-focus goals and give yourself a motivating example of what you'll notice when you achieve that goal. ☐

- Stay focused during boring classes
- Remember what I learn in class or read so that I can use it for my homework
- Follow all parts of directions
- Remember instructions, assignments, and tasks I need to do

- Keep track of my things and what I need to do for home and school
- Return the calls or messages I receive
- Resist distractions
- Meet assignments by due date
- Be on time
- Pay attention to the time so that I won't have to rush at the last minute
- Wake up on time
- Be organized in my notebooks, computer files, desk, and/or backpack
- Finish homework efficiently each night

Here are two examples:

Goal: *Stay focused during boring classes so that I wouldn't have to waste so much time getting notes from my friends.*

What will improve: *I'd be able to do the assignments better because I'd know the information I need to do the homework. I'd have more free time!*

Goal: *Getting up when the alarm rings. I keep pushing the snooze option on my phone and fall back asleep even after my parents wake me.*

What will improve?: *I'll get up on time and get everything together that I need for school, have some breakfast, and not get my parents and teachers mad because I'm late.*

Sparking Your Synapses

From the strategies suggested below to build your attention-focus goals, write down a few of the ones you'll try. Leave a space to come back and congratulate yourself for (and record) the ones that worked! 📝

- Make sure your goal has personal value to you to keep your brain effort up.
- Break down a big goal into specific, simpler ones that you will achieve on the way to the big goal.
- Plan your first steps en route to your goal and when you'll take action on them *today*—don't procrastinate.
- Write down one or several things you'll notice as you start achieving your goal.
- Bring a notecard with the date and class name to each class. On it, you'll write the details about assignments. Keep these in the binder you bring home.
- Evaluate, then write the big idea of what your desired goal is and what you'll achieve when you reach it.
- Keep a written record of your goals for each project, class, habit to change, or skill to build. Consider posting big goals on your wall to remind your brain to stay motivated.
- Make schedules when planning long-term projects that include goal setting and time management.
- Write down to whom you can go to for help when you are stuck about how to focus your attention.
- Keep up your good attention focus habits and periodically self-check to see if you're using your plans to achieve your goals.

What Boosted Your Brainpower?

You can use these questions as guides for your self-evaluation, or choose your own reflection questions.

- What did I do that was the best use of my time?
- What improvement did I first notice?
- What did I try that I'd do again?
- What would I do differently next time?
- What other strategy from this key do I think will boost my brainpower?

You can create a chart like this one to help you in your evaluation.

Date	Strategy I Tried	What I Noticed
Day 1		
Day 2		
Day 3		
Day 4		
Day 5		

Key 5

Replacing Multitasking with Single-Tasking

It's single-tasking, not multitasking, that saves time.

WIIFY?

- Finishing the work you have to do in less time
- Enjoying more free time to do what you want to do
- Experiencing happier parents
- Relaxing by not feeling scattered
- Indulging in more sleep
- Remembering and getting more out of the homework you do

Gray Matter

Our ancestors needed single focus to stay alive in their unpredictable world. The survival-in-the-wild brain we humans inherited from them still can't do more than a single task at once, so it continually switches between separate tasks.

What feels like doing two things at once is really the brain shifting its processing from one neural network to another. Each shift comes at the cost of time and mental effort. Milliseconds are wasted when your brain has to turn off the active network and turn on the next one. This not only costs you time (which adds up) but also depletes your brain's critical resources like glucose and oxygen . . . and you remember less.

Setting the Stage for Success

Think in advance of what you'll be able to do with the time you free up when you reduce the brainpower drain of multitasking and finish your work much sooner. Also enjoy the bonus of your parents not being able to nag you about doing what you want before bed because you'll have finished your homework!

Brain Boosters

It's understandable that doing homework is less of a drudge when you combine it with talking or texting with friends, or watching television. But if you want to complete all your assignments and have more free time, single-tasking is for you.

Here are strategies teens have found helpful to limit the brain drain of multitasking:

- Turn off social media, messaging, and email.
- Silence your phone.
- Eliminate television.
- Stop video game play, except for planned breaks.
- Keep a healthy snack and water nearby so that you won't have to leave your work area.
- Limit off-topic web browsing when your homework involves the Internet. If you're tempted to go to a link that is not on task, bookmark it and visit it when time permits.
- Set a timer for regular breaks—about twenty minutes of focused work, then a five-minute break. (Physical activity is always a brain-boosting break, but it's your choice.)

The outcome of multitasking is that more time is expended doing two things together than the total time it would take to do each task individually. By using strategies to avoid the distractions that cause you to multitask, you can achieve more in less time.

Sparking Your Synapses

If you want to see if your multitasking is cutting into your free time, keep a record of time spent on homework for a few days. On some days follow your normal routine, and on a few, avoid the multitasking reduction of your brain's efficiency—don't mix homework with your social media, texting, checking email, talking with friends, or too frequent snack or TV breaks.

You can make a chart like this in your notebook to track your time spent. If you'd like, you can rate the quality of your work on a scale from 1 to 5, with 5 being the highest quality.

Day	Single-tasking or Multitasking?	Start Time	End Time	Total Time	Quality Rating

What Boosted Your Brainpower?

You can use these questions as guides for your self-evaluation, or choose your own reflection questions.

- What did I do that was the best use of my time?
- What improvement did I first notice?
- What did I try that I'd do again?
- What would I do differently next time?

- What other strategy from this key do I think will boost my brainpower?

You can create a chart like this one to help you in your evaluation.

Date	Strategy I Tried	What I Noticed
Day 1		
Day 2		
Day 3		
Day 4		
Day 5		

DOOR TWO

PLANNING AND ORGANIZING

These skills allow you to manage your time to get through all you need to do, completely and successfully, each day and each month. Knowing what tasks are most important to your final goal and setting priorities are both critical in this area. When you can keep track of assignments, supplies, and information, you can use your valuable time to do the required work, instead of scrambling to get ready. You'll accomplish more, accurately and more quickly. Imagine what you could do with all the hours you'll free up!

Key 6

Working Smarter, Not Harder

*Organization isn't something you were born with,
but you can build your brainpower to do the work
you need to do—and do it well, on time,
and in less time.*

WIIFY?

- Keeping track of what you need to do and getting it done on time
- Being prompt and not having to rush at the last minute
- Being organized in your notebooks, binders, computer files, desk, and backpack
- Finishing your homework efficiently—and doing even better work in less time
- Remembering what you need to bring home or to school
- Accurately following instructions, assignments, and directions

Gray Matter

Your body has limits to the amount of physical energy you can exert, such as how much weight you can lift or how fast you can run, depending on your state of physical fitness. Just as you can increase your physical strength by exercising, you can also increase the amount of work your brain accomplishes with the mental energy you have.

When you've already been successful at a skill or task, your brain is wired to be more optimistic about taking on related challenges. You'll increase your brain's energy investment in powering up for better organization skills by recognizing those organization strategies and systems you've already developed and now use successfully.

Setting the Stage for Success

This list can give you some ideas about things you might already have organized. As you think about those things, consider what system you used and how you keep the organization updated.

- Music on your playlists
- Addresses, email, and phone numbers
- Collections
- Photos
- Special mementos
- Favorite books or recorded music

Brain Boosters

In addition to having created some of your own organizational systems, it's likely that you've also seen good organizational systems and strategies in your daily life. By thinking about ones that are familiar, you can discover strategies you'll be able to apply to organizing your own life.

Look through the examples here and pause at the ones that are familiar to you. Write down your ideas about how those are organized.

Then think a bit about how you could organize each differently, and write down what you would change to make it better or more useful to you. Remember, there is no right or wrong way to organize. The only criterion for good organization is if it works for *you*!

- *Textbooks*—Is the book divided into chapters that demonstrate good sequence and separate information into useful topics? What do you find particularly well designed for your use; for example, are the table of contents, definitions, index, and links to other resources all placed in good sequences?
- *The school year/vacation schedule*—Do the vacation breaks overlap with holidays when families are likely to travel? Does the planning allow for the school year to be broken into chunks so you get frequent enough breaks? Would it be better to have a shorter summer vacation and more frequent weeklong breaks throughout the year? Should breaks be planned before final exams so that you can study, or after exams so that you can really relax?
- *Season schedule for a sports team*—Are the games with any one opponent spread across the season to allow a team who is not playing well at the beginning enough time to improve? Is there enough of a break, especially after long travel days, for players to be fully rested for final and playoff games?
- *The classification of plants and animals (kingdom, phylum, class, order, family, genus, species)*—Most biologists find the current classifications, such as what distinguishes a plant from an animal or an amphibian from a reptile, to be very effective because the characteristics that identify the members of the group are clearly listed and identifiable. What can you learn from these classifications that would help you put your own things, like documents on your computer, into folders with clearly identifiable characteristics? For example, would photos of you playing your sport belong in your soccer folder or in your folder of photos from the current year?
- *Someone you know who is organized*—A teacher, friend, sibling, or parent, for example, can also be a good source of ideas. What does that person do to stay organized? If you don't know, observe them or ask them.

As you write down all the strategies you've observed and add your own ideas for making them better, you'll be designing your own personalized organizing toolkit. You can add to your toolkit from the strategies suggested below. Select and write a few words about ones you'd like to try. If you want to supercharge this brain booster to be even more powerful, write about how you'll use the strategy in the next few days. ✏

- Prepare a set of note cards to take to school each day to fill in new assignments and due dates: what you need to bring home and things you need to bring to school the next day for that class.
- Use color-coded folders or note cards to organize what you need for each class and project. Store these in a designated file drawer in your room, or name and color-code folders on your computer.
- Use your smartphone, computer, or tablet's reminder program or datebook to organize and keep track of your due dates for assignments, sports practice and games, club meetings, plans with family and friends, and anything else you plan to do.
- Keep a master list of the names of all your active files (computer or paper). Once a month, remove items no longer needed from each folder and the master list.
- Attach a pen and sticky-note dispenser to your desk. If you have a landline phone, keep a set of these items attached to a surface near that as well so that you'll always be prepared to write down information about plans and appointments you make.
- When you receive information verbally about something you need to do and can't immediately write it down, do something that will remind you about that information at a time when you can. For example, move something you usually wear out of its regular place—switch your fitness band to the other wrist or put your ring on another finger. When you come to a place where you can write down what you needed to remember, noticing your fitness band or ring will alert you that there is information you need to remember.

- Even with your organizational systems and lists, it's great to have a final reminder object you'll always see right before leaving your room or house—perhaps a lamp or poster in your room; the last thing you use in the bathroom, like your hairbrush; or your backpack. Affix a small pad to that object and write down the things you need to bring with you the next time you leave. Make a habit of looking at it before leaving.
- Keep a list that includes strategies that worked and when to use them. For example,

Strategy I'll try: *Color-coding so that I can keep my work organized by subject and project.*

What I'll do: *Use color-coded folders in my file drawer and as my computer desktop folders. I'll include the subject or project name and date on each.*

Sparking Your Synapses

Getting ready in the morning is a problem for many teens. A morning organization system can help you avoid that scattered start to your day. You'll find the day is much less stressful as you bring everything you need, have time for breakfast, and don't have anyone bugging you about being late.

1. Prepare a master list of everything you might need to do and bring to school on *any* day for both in-school and afterschool activities; for example, pens, pencils, homework (include each subject on your list), morning chores, packing lunch, removing things from your backpack and binder that need to stay at home, and packing special items such as sports gear or permission slips.
2. For the next three school days, use the list to organize and prepare successfully for what you need to do each day. Go through it when you first get home from school, again in the evening before going to bed, and make a final check before leaving for school.

3. After the three days, try this to see the success you've already achieved in building a stronger brain network to direct your daily organization. Without looking at your master list, write down all the items on it you can remember. When you finish, compare the two lists—and give yourself credit for those you remembered.

As you continue to practice your new organizational skills, they'll eventually become automatic routines helping you stay on top of assignments, projects, and plans. You can continue to use the list or make the list shorter and shorter as more of the items become habits.

What Boosted Your Brainpower?

You can use these questions as guides for your self-evaluation, or choose your own reflection questions.

- What did I do that was the best use of my time?
- What improvement did I first notice?
- What did I try that I'd do again?
- What would I do differently next time?
- What other strategy from this key do I think will boost my brainpower?

You can create a chart like this one to help you in your evaluation.

Date	Strategy I Tried	What I Noticed
Day 1		
Day 2		
Day 3		
Day 4		
Day 5		

Key 7

Using Visual Organizers

*Visual organizers can help your brain cluster
information that belongs together.*

WIIFY?

- Keeping information organized in your brain
- Using less mental energy to remember things
- Following your organization plans more easily by using an external storage system

Gray Matter

Your brain loves patterns. It began looking for patterns when you were born, and those patterns became guides to get things you wanted and to understand new things you heard, saw, smelled, touched, and felt.

For starters, as a baby, each time you cried and got something that made you feel better, your brain recognized a pattern: that crying brings comfort, food, or a dry diaper. As a result, you became more efficient at crying. As you grew and experienced more relationships, your brain constructed more patterns, such

41

as connecting the "moo" sound with cows, boxes with wrapping and bows as presents for you, and perhaps early associations of green mushy foods and yucky taste.

There are so many situations, questions, feelings, and choices the brain must evaluate and respond to all day long. It would be impossible to get through a day, or even an hour, unless the brain had a storage system of patterns and relationships to go to in order to react automatically and appropriately to honking horns, ringing phones, flashing lights, and smells of electrical fires, as well as smells of grilling burgers.

Throughout your life, you've been building your own storage system, your pattern and relationship memory library, as you repeatedly experience certain things together. Your brain instantaneously accesses this library of associations to interpret the world around you. Thanks to this library, you don't have to reevaluate the meaning of your alarm each time it awakens you in the morning or figure out how to use a toothbrush each time you want to brush your teeth.

By matching your brain's natural tendency to construct strong memories based on clearly identified patterns, visual organizers hook perfectly into its organization system.

Setting the Stage for Success

Look at this list of systems that are forms of visual organizers. It's likely that you already use some of them. By thinking about how these work to keep information or procedures linked together, you'll preheat your brain circuits to construct your own visual organizers to serve you as guidance and planning systems.

- Maps are visual organizers used to plot travel plans.
- Graphs are visual organizers that display related information for easier comparison.
- Checklists used by pilots, coaches, party planners, and others who repeatedly need to follow the same multiple steps are visual organizers used to plan and prepare.
- Diagrams with labels, such as labels on the parts of the body or names of people in a photograph, are visual organizers to guide recognition of these items each time the diagram or photo is viewed.

Brain Boosters

In creating visual organizers to classify things you choose in an orderly, sequential, or systematic way, you can start by selecting from a variety of styles. As you look at these examples, think about which might be helpful for things you want to organize in your life. Write down the types of organizers by name or draw an example of a few of the graphics you think could be useful and label them with the particular task or system for which they would be helpful organizers. ☐

Flowchart

Flowcharts are great for things that need to be organized with a step-by-step plan.

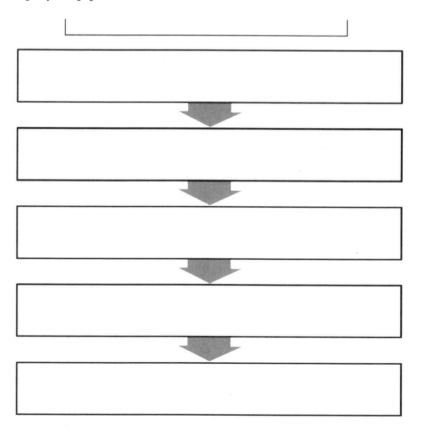

The first line is the name of what you want to get and keep organized, such as the files on your computer. The arrows indicate the order in which you need to get your documents prepared so that they'll be organized now and ready for use as you go.

1. Make a master folder and pull into it all the files you want to organize.
2. After looking at the various types of information you have, make individual folders with category names. These category names and the items in each folder are just preliminary, so the sorting of what goes where or what you call the folders is not critical at this point.
3. Drag the files from your master folder into the category folders you made.
4. Now go through each category folder and remove files that don't really fit with the others. Put these back into the original master folder.
5. After trimming down your category folders so that they no longer have the unrelated files, you can change their names to something easy to identify, arrange the files in an order that is useful, or make subfolders for smaller categories within the folder.
6. Return to the master folder and go back to step 2 as you make new category folders for those remaining files that didn't fit well into the first set of categories.

Sandwich

Sandwiches are organized ways to group a number of food items so they stay together for you to eat. When there are clusters of things you need to do to be organized for a task and the order doesn't matter, use a sandwich as your visual organizer.

For example, if you frequently have to pack a sports bag to take to games or practice, the sandwich visual organizer could have headgear as the top bread, footwear as the bottom bread, and other items you need (such as balls, snacks, a water bottle, your uniform, and a towel) as the layers between the slices of bread.

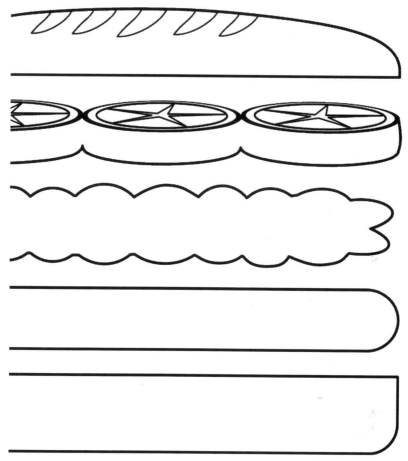

Sandwich Graphic Organizer
Paul Willis

Timelines

A timeline is a visual map of things that need to be done during whatever time period you have to complete the task. Use time-lines when the specific things in a repeating task are generally the same, such as the number of pages you need to read each night to finish a book in time for a book report. Or you might record your plan of what you'll do each day over a five-day period as you prepare for a final exam or do a research report. Although the specific tasks (books to read and tests to review) will be different each time, you can reuse the visual organizer over and over by just writing in the specific dates each time above the tasks that remain the same.

Timeline Example:
Reading a book by a required completion date

Date	Date	Date	Date	Date
Pages to read	Pages to read	Pages to read	Pages to read	Pages to read

-----------------|----------------------|----------------------|----------------------|-----------------è

Sparking Your Synapses

Visual organizers are guides or maps directing your brain to easily know what to do for tasks that come up repeatedly. Select a task where you'd benefit from being better organized, and choose a visual organizer style you'd like to try to simplify that task and your life.

Now that you know your brain loves and remembers things best when the patterns are evident, you'll find more and more ways to simplify your life (and have more free time) by using visual organizers. The bonus is that the more often you use a visual organizer you create for a particular task, such as planning a book report or keeping track of all the items you need to bring to a sports event, the more your brain strengthens that pattern of information.

As is always the case with your neuroplasticity, *practice makes permanent*, and you'll often find you no longer need to refer to your visual organizer as your brain learns to follow it automatically.

What Boosted Your Brainpower?

You can use these questions as guides for your self-evaluation, or choose your own reflection questions. ☞

- What did I do that was the best use of my time?
- What improvement did I first notice?
- What did I try that I'd do again?
- What would I do differently next time?
- What other strategy from this key do I think will boost my brainpower?

You can create a chart like this one to help you in your evaluation.

Date	Strategy I Tried	What I Noticed
Day 1		
Day 2		
Day 3		
Day 4		
Day 5		

Key 8

Planning, Not Scrambling

*When you become skilled at prioritizing,
you'll regain control of your free time without guilt
or pressure about tasks you "should" be doing.*

WIIFY?

- Completing daily homework in less time and boosting its quality
- Turning in papers and projects when they are due
- Creating a plan for breaking long-term tasks into doable daily steps
- Saving time by having all your work for reports, projects, and jobs together and in the same place so that they're easy to find
- Not missing appointments, meetings, deadlines, release of ticket sales, or dates with friends

Gray Matter

Prioritizing is the executive function that guides you when you plan an essay, project, or report, or plan your day, week, and year. Think about a project where 90 percent of the grade is based on content and only 10 percent is based on graphics, cover, diagrams, and artwork. It might be more fun to do the design components, and some teens would do that first and end up spending lots of time on those parts of the project. When too little time is left to do the less interesting, but more highly valued work on the content, the end result is more glitter than substance, and grades suffer.

Your brain also uses its prioritizing skills when you separate less relevant details from the main ideas of a text, analyze word problems in math, select what lecture information to include in notes, and decide what material to study for a test. Good prioritizing skills will guide you to make the most of your time because you'll know which information is most valuable and plan accordingly. When you make these choices thoughtfully, you'll have more successful outcomes in less time.

Setting the Stage for Success

Remind your neurons about the successful prioritizing that they've already done by taking credit for any of these prioritizing tasks:

- Selecting your choices of which television programs to prerecord
- Choosing items to pack for a trip when you only have a small bag or backpack
- Narrowing down the group of friends you invite to your birthday party when the activity or location can involve only a limited number
- Picking the most important information to study for a test on which you made great choices and aced the exam

Heighten your brain's positive expectations and goal-directed efforts further by taking time to think about things you don't have enough time for now but will be able to do when you efficiently plan your time to get the most out of your effort.

Brain Boosters

As you develop the skill of prioritizing, you'll be able to plan your schedule to match your brain's peak brainpower surges. You'll know which tasks are the highest priority and break the habit of putting off the ones you like least, but that count the most, and not doing your best as a result. 🖯

- Make a list of all the parts of an assignment, project, long-term plan, or big goal. Just write down the tasks as they come to mind, and then revise your list in the order in which things should be done.
- Next to each item, write stars to indicate the importance or value of that task to the final outcome or grade.
- Write estimates for the time you predict each task will take.
- Know when you do your best work and plan your schedule accordingly. Plan to do "high value" tasks that are particularly difficult for a time when your brain is at its best (for example, first thing after school, or after some exercise, or before others come home and the house is noisy).
- Create visual organizers (like the table below) to prioritize how you'll divide your time *before* starting a long-term project or for planning a study schedule for final exams. Schedule your time allotments based on your rating of the importance of that task.

To prioritize information—that is, to emphasize what you need to remember from a lecture or textbook reading, or what to study for a test—you can use the approach of a news reporter. This familiar nursery rhyme will show you how it works:

Jack and Jill went up the hill to fetch a pail of water.
Jack fell down and broke his crown
And Jill came tumbling after.

- Who? *Jack and Jill*
- When? *Not known*
- What? *A fall*

- Where? *A hill*
- How? *Using pails*
- Why? *To get water*
- What is the important message? *When on top of a high place, watch where you step.*

Now use the same system to recognize the most important information to remember from a short topic section from one of your textbooks or literature reading assignments. To guide your brain to seek out this information, write down the seven questions in a list before you start to read. Either as you read or when you finish the section, write down your responses. ▷

Each time you try this strategy, your brain will become more efficient at recognizing high-priority material.

Sparking Your Synapses

Your homework is a great place to start using these prioritizing strategies; use them to plan long-term projects and goals. Take into account which tasks are most valuable and which should be done early as you plan the amount of time and the order in which you'll do each day's assignments.

For your homework assignments today or tomorrow, copy down the visual organizer below (or create your own version of it). Fill in the information as designated in the spaces for each subject ▷

1. List the tasks to be done to complete the assignment for each subject, including any items you need to bring in the next day.
2. Rate each task from 1 to 5 to indicate its importance to the final outcome or grade.
3. Write down how much time you think you'll need for each task. Take into consideration the rating of importance you assigned to the task.

4. Plan your full homework schedule:

- Put the subjects in the order you prioritize as best to do first; use your estimates to write in predicted start and finish time.
- Include five-minute breaks after about twenty to thirty minutes of focused work time. These planned breaks will reduce your temptation to interrupt your work to respond to texts, check your email, or lose efficiency with other distractions.
- Setting the timer for your estimated finish time will keep you on track so that you don't overspend time on low-value tasks and run out before doing the high-value ones.

Today's Date _____

Subject	What I Have to Do	Importance of Task (1–5)	Estimated Amount of Time Needed	Estimated Start Time	Break	Estimated Finish Time

You can use a similar table for prioritizing in advance of future long-term projects or planning study schedules for big exams.

The brain gets a pleasure reward when it recognizes success. Also, when you give it insights about how to be more successful (e.g., what you did that worked and what you'd change), it grabs on to these as keys to obtain the pleasure it seeks. So power up your brain's prioritizing skills by going back to the homework plans you prepared and followed for a few days, and think about how things went.

What Boosted Your Brainpower?

You can use these questions as guides for your self-evaluation, or choose your own reflection questions.

- What did I do that was the best use of my time?
- What improvement did I first notice?
- What did I try that I'd do again?
- What would I do differently next time?
- What other strategy from this key do I think will boost my brainpower?

You can create a chart like this one to help you in your evaluation.

Date	Strategy I Tried	What I Noticed
Day 1		
Day 2		
Day 3		
Day 4		
Day 5		

Key 9

Keeping Up Long-Term Effort

*Developing a lifelong habit of perseverance
will help you achieve your goals.*

WIIFY?

- Sticking to your plans to complete long-term assignments successfully
- Following through on commitments
- Staying with tasks long enough to finish
- Avoiding burnout
- Having more free time as a result of boosting your effort to complete things you have to do

Gray Matter

Your brain is still building its executive function skill of perseverance that powers you to sustain effort for long-term goals. Even if you really want to do the things you know are important (to you or your parents) like getting good grades, taking the most challenging AP (Advanced Placement) or IB (International

Baccalaureate) courses, doing community service, or reading books instead of playing video games, the neural networks used to achieve those goals are still under construction.

From neuroscience research, we've learned that the brain puts in greater effort over longer periods of time when it has the expectation that there are doable smaller steps along the way to a more distant final goal. When the brain has expectations of the pleasure response to progress achieved, it will keep taking those steps as it keeps getting evidence of progress.

The brain's internal response to the awareness that it has achieved success is a spike in dopamine, a neurochemical that produces feelings of deep pleasure and satisfaction. These feelings strongly motivate the brain to keep going, take on the challenge of the next level, and enjoy the next warm wave of internal satisfaction.

Setting the Stage for Success

The best video games, the ones that hook players for hours, do so by giving frequent motivating information (feedback) about a player's goal progress. Let's say a game has ten levels, each with a task or skill that players must achieve or master in order to move up to the next level. If this game showed the players their progress only after they spent hours completing *all* the levels, no one would play it.

What makes video games so compelling is the way they continuously give players evidence that their practice and continued efforts are effective. Whether it's banners, bells, or a change in background or sound effects, as each level is completed, players receive progress feedback.

The same progress-feedback-pleasure system is what kept you going when you built new skills, even when there were lots of struggles at first. When you learned to keyboard, skateboard, snowboard, play an instrument, or kick a soccer ball, you received ongoing evidence that you were getting better the more you practiced.

Even though you knew you had not yet reached your goal of being fully proficient and skilled at the task, the *frequent feedback of progress* sustained your continued effort, in spite of falls, setbacks, and mistakes.

This is the same system of motivation and sustained effort you'll tap into when you use feedback, such as goal-progress tracking, to inform your brain of the progress you are making along the path to achieving your final goals. Each time your brain gets the feedback that you're progressing toward a goal, the achievement response makes your brain feel a bit more capable and optimistic about more success. You'll be building up your brainpower of perseverance that keeps effort up for the long-term, even after setbacks, failures, and extraordinary challenges.

Brain Boosters

When you need to do something challenging, you can inspire your reluctant brain to continue putting forth the effort needed by making sure it gets glimpses of progress with feedback strategies like these:

- Try to think of some ways that the required goal can provide you with a personal goal—something you want. What could you look forward to doing with the skill you are building physically, musically, or recreationally (for example, visiting the country where your foreign language is spoken)? How might the information you're required to learn help you in a future career?
- Before you can get feedback for progress en route to a final goal, you need to have a system for recognizing that progress. It won't be automatic, like seeing the clear evidence as your guitar playing or ball-handling skills gradually improved. For those assigned long-term tasks, reports, projects, or proficiency goals, start by writing a checklist (or visual organizer) including each step you need to complete. For example:

If the goal is to read a 200-page book in a month, write down the ten pages you'll read on each of twenty days during the month. Plot it out so that you can get the progress-feedback-pleasure from crossing out each segment of reading as you complete it.

If the goal is memorizing thirty geometry theorems (or rivers, mountain ranges, and lakes in a country, or formulas for physics), create a bar, like a thermometer, and mark off ten progress points you'll achieve on the way to thirty. As you reach each progressive mark, color in that additional space. You'll be giving your brain the visual feedback it loves each time you create that evidence of progress.

- Effort-to-progress graphs are another type of visual organizer you can use to build your brain's perseverance. This graph came from an eleventh-grade student whose goal was to get better at sinking foul shots in basketball. At each practice session, he took twenty-five shots and recorded the number he got in. After each session, he repeated the same evaluation. He also recorded the cumulative time he had put into practicing; that is, he added the time of each day's practice to the total time he had practiced so far.

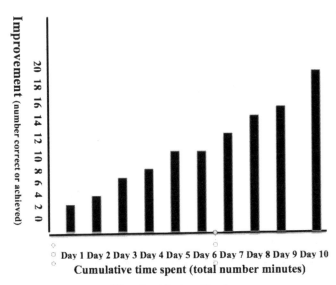

Effort-Goal Project Graph

The graph provides visible evidence that the more *effort* he put in (time he practiced), the more *progress* he made in achieving a greater number of successful foul shots.

Sparking Your Synapses

Select something you need to do this week or month that you dread because it's time-consuming, boring, or too difficult. Choose a goal with progress you can measure with a number; for example, the accurate foul shots in the graph above, the number of drawers you organize in your room, the total number of vocabulary words you learned in a foreign language (this could be measured by having the words on flash cards with translations on the back and counting the number correct), or the total number of lines memorized in a school play script.

Set up a graph and label the vertical axis with numbers suited to how your progress will be measured (for example, the number of vocabulary words you correctly define). Label the horizontal axis with a measure of amount of total time spent, adding each day's time to the sum of the times from all the previous days.

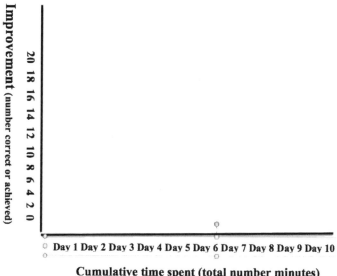

Your Effort-Goal Project Graph

What Boosted Your Brainpower?

You can use these questions as guides for your self-evaluation, or choose your own reflection questions. 📑

- What did I do that was the best use of my time?
- What improvement did I first notice?
- What did I try that I'd do again?
- What would I do differently next time?
- What other strategy from this key do I think will boost my brainpower?

You can create a chart like this one to help you in your evaluation.

Date	Strategy I Tried	What I Noticed
Day 1		
Day 2		
Day 3		
Day 4		
Day 5		

DOOR THREE
MANAGING YOUR EMOTIONS

When you master these keys, you'll be in charge of your emotions rather than being controlled by them. You'll learn to check in and evaluate your emotional state, recognize stress, and use strategies to reduce it. With your brain maintaining its cool, you'll discover how much more you'll remember, understand, and get done. You'll stress out less about friends and enjoy more pleasurable time with family and on your own.

Key 10

Navigating Your Brain's Emotional Highways

*Understanding the automatic system that blocks your
control of your emotional responses will help you
build a detour around stress-induced roadblocks.*

WIIFY?

- Understanding why you get stressed out
- Knowing your specific sources of stresses
- Responding calmly when you are hurt, angry, or frustrated
- Feeling less irritable, with fewer mood swings
- Keeping your temper

Gray Matter

Until your executive function networks develop more fully, your emotional response system operates much like that of mammals in the wild, where quick responses are critical for survival.

This quick survival response system is located, not high in your thinking prefrontal cortex, but rather lower in the brain where signals are automatic and involuntary. When you are anxious, sad, frustrated, bored, hurt, or angry, your survival reactions take over. This automatic system's responses are limited to variations of the fight, flight, or freeze reactions seen in animals when they are stressed (for example, by being trapped) or perceive threat. The human variations to these instinctive reactions include rage, withdrawing, yelling, saying hurtful things, and risk taking.

In order for your executive function networks to keep you in charge of your emotional self-management, they must send messages to the rest of the brain beyond their network in your prefrontal cortex. Problems occur when the communications from these prefrontal cortex networks are hindered from reaching the lower brain.

The roadblock takes place deep in your brain where a structure redirects brain traffic flow when you are stressed, fearful, upset, or anxious. The structure is called the *amygdala*. When you are experiencing high stress, the amygdala becomes highly activated, uses a lot of brain energy, and blocks the flow of information into and out of your prefrontal cortex. When the stressed amygdala cuts off communications from your self-control executive functions, it redirects control to your lower brain. At that point, your automatic survival system takes control of what you say and do.

Examples of your lower brain taking control occur when you are so bored (yes, long periods of boredom are stressful to your brain) that you lose track of what you are reading and your brain drifts to something else or when you say hurtful things in anger to someone who bumped you by accident.

Setting the Stage for Success

Remember, to get your brain to put in the effort to grow the powers you want it to build, you must believe success is a possibility. To boost your brain's expectations that you can change, it is important to know that things you've done or said in a high-stress state, with your low brain in control, were *not* your voluntary choices.

By thinking about times when stress put your low brain in charge—perhaps because you were anxious, sad, frustrated, bored, hurt, or angry—you'll be gathering an inventory of awareness about things you did not choose to do. That doesn't mean you can do any of these things and not have to take responsibility. The goal of building your awareness of these reactive responses, when your thinking brain could not control your actions, is to avoid the pessimistic surrender that accompanies feelings of personal inadequacy.

Look at this list of reactions that are typical involuntary responses to stress. Select ones that you have experienced when stress took over and you regretted the outcome. Write down a few of the ones you've experienced. ☐

- Cheating on a test
- Yelling at someone
- Telling lies
- Damaging school or public property
- Breaking rules
- Blaming others for bad things you did or bad choices you made
- Pretending to be sick
- Emotional outbursts
- Ignoring safety precautions
- Failing to stand up for someone being bullied
- Copying someone's homework
- Taking someone's property
- Teasing or saying hurtful things

With the optimistic realization that you can change from involuntary reactive behavior to thoughtful, reflective responses to stress and strong emotions, your brain will be ready to put in the effort and use the strategies that follow.

Brain Boosters

High stress cuts off your brain's control of your actions, which are no longer your choice. To others, it may appear as if you are choosing to be lazy, irresponsible, or intentionally disruptive, or even that you have low intelligence or a neurological disorder hyperactivity disorder.

When they are reacting in a state of stress, teens often hear untrue statements like these:

- Teens are scattered because they are lazy and self-absorbed.
- If you have trouble paying attention, something is wrong with your brain.
- Goofing off is willful disobedience, and if you just try harder, you would do better.
- I did just fine in my day, so there is no reason today's teenagers can't get it together.
- You have to make do with the brain you were born with.
- There are certain things boys can't do as well as girls and others girls can't do as well as boys.

You need a math brain to do math. Now that you know that your behavior and choices in the stress-state may result in negative reactions from others, let's make plans to keep that from happening. Think of something for which you've been repeatedly criticized (which you now know is not the real "you"). For example:

- Trying to pay attention, but losing focus when you're stressed by hunger, tiredness, or emotional turmoil.
- Answering questions wrong when you are asked in front of the whole class, even though you know the answers, because you're nervous.
- Not remembering to do an assignment or task you had planned to do, because your reactive brain was all caught up in a fight you had with your friend or parents, or because you were upset by something someone said to you or about you.

Write down what you do in a stress state that results in criticism. Then write down the incorrect impressions people make about you because they think you are in voluntary brain control and therefore choosing that action or behavior. Next, plan your action so that you can activate it even when you're stressed. Although high stress blocks optimal communication between your high and low brains, there is still information going through those circuits—just not as well or as helpfully. When you give your upper brain advance notice about something that reduces its control and work out a strategy that is ready to use when stress takes over, you'll be able to reduce the criticisms based on incorrect assumptions about your choices. ▱

Here's how it may look, based on the first example:

- Your action: *Trying to pay attention, but losing focus when you're stressed by hunger, tiredness, or emotional turmoil.*
- Incorrect impressions: *You don't care about learning; you're too lazy to put in the effort; or you're a scattered person who does not have ability to focus your attention.*
- Advance plan: You know which physical or emotional triggers switch your brain into survival mode. Plan the words you could use to explain that you're not yourself today because you didn't have breakfast (or get enough sleep or are upset about an argument you had, etc.).

Sparking Your Synapses

To take action, you need to believe that things can change. When you stop taking all the blame for some of the bad choices or actions that took place when your brain was not under your voluntary control, you can move forward to a brain state that enhances self-awareness, thoughtful responses, and responsible decisions. Your emotional self-awareness will blossom.

Using this chart, write down the specific responses to stress you've experienced, and add any others you think of. By writing down what you recognize as the stress categories that have impacted you, you'll be directing your brain to these as "priority goals." ▱

Stressor	Your Response
Rejection anxiety	Not doing things your friends might think are not cool, such as sitting with people you'd like to be with who are not in your "group," or standing up for someone being teased by your friends

Stressor	Your Response
Embarrassment	Not participating in discussions, fear of making mistakes
Frustration about test failures or fear of the low grades	Cheating on a test
Confusion so stressful it blocked your attention focus	Falling even further behind
Fear of the consequences of something you did accidentally	Blaming someone else
Being upset by something someone did or said to you	Pretending to be sick to avoid facing that person in school

What Boosted Your Brainpower?

You can use these questions as guides for your self-evaluation, or choose your own reflection questions.

- What did I do that was the best use of my time?
- What improvement did I first notice?
- What did I try that I'd do again?
- What would I do differently next time?
- What other strategy from this key do I think will boost my brainpower?

You can create a chart like this one to help you in your evaluation.

Date	Strategy I Tried	What I Noticed
Day 1		
Day 2		
Day 3		
Day 4		
Day 5		

Key 11

Preventing Your Emotions from Taking Control

*When you find your emotional temperature rising,
you can calm yourself with some simple techniques.*

WIIFY?

- Recognizing when your stress levels are rising and knowing when to take action before stress blocks your control of your emotions
- Having a toolkit of easy, effective practices you can use to quickly reduce stress
- Keeping your cool instead of hitting the emotional red zone
- Getting rid of the baggage you've been carrying from feeling blame or guilt about actions that were driven by your reactive, survival brain and were not your voluntary choices

Gray Matter

You could have the best professional telescope for viewing a lunar eclipse or an app that gives you an hour's head start on pre-release concert tickets, but if you don't know when the eclipse will take place or the concert tickets will go on sale, your tools won't have much value.

That simple truth applies to managing stress as well. Once you've developed greater awareness of your emotional states and of what situations are most likely to push up your stress levels, your brain is primed for building emotional self-management tools.

Research has shown that students who developed and practiced self-calming strategies to keep control of their emotional responses improved their attention, focus, concentration, memory, and test performance. You'll build self-calming skills into your brain's memory networks by practicing them. The more you practice these mental exercises, the more easily accessible they'll be when you want to slow down rushing thoughts and stressful feelings.

Setting the Stage for Success

When have you been aware of your emotional state becoming increasingly negative and done something to retake control of how you were feeling? Here are some examples that may remind you of your emotional perception and positive action.

- When thinking about an upcoming test, you got so stressed you couldn't even concentrate on studying. You felt you were too far behind for it to do any good. You went for a walk, played with your dog, and felt calmer when you returned to your studies. In that calmer state, you were able to study more successfully.
- When you could not play the guitar chord or kick the soccer ball as well as others in practice, your frustration was increasing. You felt like quitting or thought you just didn't have the skills needed. You took a break or got something to drink and felt more refreshed. You then asked someone to give you some tips that you applied successfully. Instead of quitting out of frustration, you stepped away for

a time and came back with a fresher attitude so that you could ask for help.

- When your younger sister messed with your things, you immediately got angry and yelled at her. Seeing her tears, you were able to calm your anger with reassuring thoughts that she was just doing what little kids do. You turned your anger around into plans to put your things out of her reach and took out something you could play with together.

Set the stage for your success further by recognizing the successes you've already had helping others regain control of their emotions when they were spiraling out of control. Perhaps you've been with a small child who was close to having a tantrum because he wanted something he couldn't have or didn't seem to want to play with any of the toys you offered. What did you do to restore his calm—and preserve your sanity? If you've never been in that situation, it's likely there are others, so think about those.

Brain Boosters

The first step to controlling emotions is to know when your stress is building to a level that you need to prevent. One way to strengthen your early warning system is to create an accurate emotional thermometer for yourself. You'll build it by taking your emotional temperature on a scheduled basis at first. With time, it will become an automatic monitor to alert you to the need for action.

The emotions listed here are common causes of stress in teens. Make a list of the ones you've experienced that have been stressful to you. Add any other things to your list that sometimes stress you out. ✎

- Worried or anxious
- Nervous

- Bored
- Frustrated
- Angry
- Sad
- Embarrassed
- Confused
- Frightened
- Unfocused or scattered

Make a chart in your notebook or for your desk to use at home *and* make a similar one on a notecard for school listing the emotions you wrote down as being stressful to you. You might want to add an emoticon or emoji (downloaded or drawn) next to the emotion it represents.

For the next four to seven days (or until you experience and record a variety of high-stress experiences), you'll want to have something to remind you to take your emotional temperature at set times throughout the school day and at home. You can use a quiet alarm or vibrate on your watch, cell phone, or tablet that you will have with you wherever you go, especially school. Set it to go off once an hour during your waking hours.

When it goes off, record the time and using your notecard, write the name or draw the face that best represents your emotional state.

- If you are feeling one of your negative states, write what you are doing or what is happening at that time.
- If it is not one of the stress states, you can just note the time and a check or describe your positive feeling.
- If you are still feeling the same negative emotion you were experiencing at your last check-in an hour ago, add an arrow to indicate if the emotion is getting stronger or less intense, or is about the same.

It takes practice to build automatic self-awareness that lets you know when your stress is building up and threatening to ambush your emotional self-control. But a week (or even less) of record keeping should allow your brain enough practice to monitor awareness of your emotional temperature to know if you should use one of the self-calming stress busters you'll learn next.

There is no single right way to do any self-calming activity, including the three described here. The main thing is to find an activity that works well and feels comfortable for you and practice it enough so that you can activate it automatically, like turning on a light switch to break the stress build-up before it takes over.

You can do these activities any time or place without anyone knowing that you're doing them. Although the practice instructions include techniques like keeping your eyes closed, ultimately, you will not need to do that if you are using the relaxing tool in class or around other people, because your private practice sessions will have made it easy for you to reach the calm state you seek.

Breathing

When building this tool, start by sitting in a private, comfortable place with your feet on the floor, eyes closed, shoulders and neck relaxed, and hands on your lap. With each breath, feel it bringing invigorating oxygen through your lungs and spreading into your arms and legs and down to your fingers and toes. As you release the breath, imagine it carrying out with it any stress it picked up as it traveled through your body. Continue for a few breaths as you feel your mind clearing. When you open your eyes, you'll notice a pleasant calmness, as well as a heightened sense of brightness and awareness.

Tense and Release

You may have noticed that you experience tightness in some parts of your body when you're stressed, perhaps your neck, back, eyes, or elsewhere. If so, this will be especially helpful for you. Start by tensing all the muscles of your body, one area at a time. Mentally go from bottom to top, starting with your toes, then foot muscles, calves, thighs, abdomen, chest, fingers, hands, forearms, upper arms, neck, jaw, eyes, and finally forehead. Hold each area tight for a few seconds, and then let all the muscle tension go. Imagine your emotional tension flowing out as your muscles release their contractions. Before opening your eyes, take a deep breath and enjoy the relaxed feeling in your body. Then notice the increased energy and emotional strength you have along with the release of the stress.

Visualizations

Find a memory of a place and time when you felt very comfortable, safe, and peaceful. If you prefer, use a photograph of a place you've been where you felt that sense of peace and calmness (or get a picture of a place that looks very peaceful).

Several times a day for a few weeks, bring the mental image to mind or look at the picture before closing your eyes and visualizing what it is like in that place. Imagine all the details of what you see as well as the sounds, smells, and sensations. Breathe slowly and deeply. When you've been in that place long enough to feel calm and energized, focus on those emotions and bring them back with you. Now you are ready to release the visualization and reconnect with renewed control and motivation to the current time and place.

Try all three of these tools, practicing one twice a day for a few days before trying the next one for the next few days. After those trial days, you'll be able to select the one (or two) that feel best for you. That is the one you'll practice twice a day for about a week (more if it doesn't yet feel automatic) so that you'll be able to access it automatically when needed.

Sparking Your Synapses

You've learned to take action in response to warning signs, such as being alerted to a possible fire when you smell something burning or see smoke. Now that you're learning the warning signs that an emotional flare-up is coming, your self-calming practice will become your brain's fire extinguishers to prevent the stress response from taking control.

Once you've found the strategies that are best for your self-calming, you'll want to be sure you can remember them and use them when they are needed in the future. To help, you can just write a brief note about specific instances where you felt stress mounting and restored your calm state by doing your breathing, muscle release, or calming visualization. ⌧

What Boosted Your Brainpower?

You can use these questions as guides for your self-evaluation, or choose your own reflection questions. ⌧

- What did I do that was the best use of my time?
- What improvement did I first notice?
- What did I try that I'd do again?
- What would I do differently next time?
- What other strategy from this key do I think will boost my brainpower?

You can create a chart like this one to help you in your evaluation.

Date	Strategy I Tried	What I Noticed
Day 1		
Day 2		
Day 3		
Day 4		
Day 5		

Key 12

Boost Your Control, Confidence, and Effectiveness

*As you break the negative habits your brain has built
to deal with frustrations, you'll find you've developed
a more comfortable mind space.*

WIIFY?

- Reducing your vulnerability to stress
- Clearing your mind of negativity and renewing your positive expectations
- Accessing a calm mental state *before* doing things that stress you out (for example, meeting new people, tryouts, tests)
- Learning to place your focus to be where you want it
- Resisting any bad habits your brain has developed
- Sleeping restfully and waking up refreshed
- Building new habits to suit your goals

Gray Matter

For most teens, the demands of increasing responsibilities frequently overwhelm their brains with stress. In addition, they often experience frustration about things that seem out of their control, such as their height, family income, comparisons to high-achieving older siblings, or the consequences of bad choices made previously when stress put the lower brain in control.

The emotional brain's quick-fix response is to temporarily reduce stress when it occurs, by impulsively doing unrelated things that feel good. Or simply, it might displace and distract you from the stress. As demands and stresses build, the quick-fix reactions multiply.

The increasing activation of the brain networks directing these stress-driven, undesirable behaviors strengthens each time they are used. Ultimately these behaviors become habits—things you do almost automatically, without thinking of the consequences. The more you fall into these negative habits, the stronger their brain networks grow and the harder they are to break. The good news is that you can gain control over the disruptive behaviors that have become distracting bad habits and replace them with healthy habits that actually do help reduce stress.

Preheating Your Brain's Positive Expectations

If you've been mentally overwhelmed by frequent and often-repeated things that stress you out, you may have found yourself turning to some of the behaviors listed below. Select the ones from either list that are relevant to you. Write them in your notebook along with an example of a negative outcome resulting from each. (For example, *zoning out in class has resulted in me not doing the right homework assignment; spending too much time on video games cuts into study time, so my test grades are low; not doing home and family chores has resulted in nagging from my parents.*)

Too much

- Television
- Zoning out in class
- Eating
- Dozing off when doing homework

- Video games
- Social media
- Listening to music in bed
- Hanging out with friends
- Sleeping

Too little

- Sticking to things that are hard or boring
- Exercise
- Keeping promises
- Doing your home and family chores
- Taking care of pets
- Keeping your room, binder, desk, and so on organized
- Sleeping

It's hard to get your brain to put big effort into something vague and huge, like stress, but being aware of specific habits that keep you from feeling and doing your best will motivate your brain to try.

Brain Boosters

By taking fifteen unplugged minutes a day, you can build up your stress resistance and start replacing the bad habits your brain has grabbed on to when it's been in the stress-survival state.

Choose three or more of the unplugged activities from the list that follows (or come up with your own) to try during the next several days. To help your brain prioritize and put the effort into trying the activities you choose, be sure they are ones that are appealing and can be done conveniently. Write down when you'll plan to do them. 🖘

Unplugged time has the greatest benefit for boosting your positive mind space if you do it soon after school or afterschool activities, and before starting homework, chores, or checking in with your social media. During these unplugged minutes, you need to be free from the Internet, phone, social media, television—essentially all things electric or mechanical.

- Draw.
- Walk through a park or take a scenic route on the way home from school.
- Sit outside on a bench or hillside overlooking a favorite view. Listen to the sounds.
- Play with pets.
- Engage in an unplugged hobby (card tricks, scrapbook, collections).
- Exercise.
- Read a favorite book.
- Think about things that are funny or fun.
- Practice a card trick or magic trick.
- Write in a journal.

Sparking the Synapses

You can copy this table with space for three days (and more if you choose) where you'll write the dates on which you'll try the unplugged activity. In the column headed Unplugged Activity, fill in the spaces with what you'll do. After completing your fifteen minutes of unplugged time each day, write down what you noticed.

Day	Unplugged Activity	What I Noticed
Monday	Played with my dog	I felt calmer and didn't rush right to my Facebook.
Day 1		
Day 2		
Day 3		

It is these positive feelings you experience from your un-plugged activities that you'll want to give your brain before you approach that which has previously triggered your stress-reactive negative habits. The more often you give your brain the positive, calm, controlled experience of the unplugged activities you practice on a regular basis, the stronger you'll build those attributes available to activate when needed to confront your challenges.

DOOR FOUR

JUDGMENT

The executive functions of judgment (including analysis and risk-assessment) allow you to resist your brain's first (impulsive) response when you're making decisions. With these skill sets, you'll be able to avoid jumping to conclusions, making choices you'll regret, or taking dangerous risks. You'll develop confidence that allows you to venture out of your comfort zone and to resist the pulls of instant gratification and peer pressure.

Key 13

Priming Your Brain to Make Wiser Decisions

Learning to resist impulsive first choices is a valuable goal.

WIIFY?

- Discovering how your brain's impulsive programming makes you jump to conclusions
- Recognizing what things push your brain to make impulsive decisions with negative consequences
- Motivating your brain to want to build the powers to override its impulsivity when you make important decisions

Gray Matter

As a teenager in today's world, you're faced with more decisions and choices than ever before. More choices may sound like a good thing, but the number of decisions you're required to make each day can overwhelm your brain at its current stage of development.

Your teen brain is programmed to be impulsive and to explore. That's a good thing when it empowers you to try new foods, to join a new club, and to extend your friendship groups. But there are times when you need to hold back on your brain's impulsivity and make important decisions that can impact the rest of your life.

You can't wait the five to ten years that is the brain's natural timeframe for creating the executive-function control systems required for the critical decisions you need to make now. The good news is that, thanks to neuroplasticity, each time you are aware of the possibility of making an impulsive decision and you use strategies to resist these choices and evaluate alternatives, the control systems you need strengthen. You can prepare your brain to make wiser decisions now.

Setting the Stage for Success

To see what you'll change when you use strategies to boost your decision-making skills, look at these frequent results you might have experienced when you made impulsive, first-response choices.

- Making careless mistakes by starting before reading all the instructions
- Rushing through reading and finding you don't remember what you read
- Choosing the first multiple-choice answer that seems right without looking at the other options that included the most correct response
- Playing video games or checking social media when you had required homework, so you had to stay up way too late or couldn't finish your homework
- Responding impulsively to a text and regretting that you didn't think about the possible negative consequences before you sent it
- Deciding early in a movie or book that a character is the bad guy, then finding out more about the person and realizing that you'd jumped to your opinion too quickly (Perhaps this has even happened in your real life!)

- Answering a call or taking a quick look at text you've been waiting for even though you are riding a bike, crossing a busy street, or driving a car
- Following along with what your friends do without considering the possible negative outcomes

Now jot down your brain-effort boosters by listing the outcome goals you'll be working for as you build your power to resist those types of impulsive choices in the future.

Brain Boosters

Answer these questions aloud one right after the other without reading ahead.

1. What color is the opposite of black?
2. What does a cow drink?

Was your immediate response to the second question "milk," even though you know that cows drink water? (Yes, calves drink milk, but the question did say "cows.") Responding "milk" is an example of the programming of your still-impulsive teen brain to stop evaluating a decision (answer) after its first response, instead of waiting to consider other options.

To see the power of goals in helping the brain resist immediate impulses, ask yourself which you'd choose: receiving $100 now or $120 in a month? Jot your answer down on a scrap of paper. Then ask yourself which you'd choose: $100 in twelve months or $120 in thirteen months?

What happened? If you're like most people, you chose to receive $100 *now* over $120 in a month. But if you're like the majority on the second question, you chose waiting out the extra month to receive $120 in thirteen months.

This is an illustration of the power of developing motivating personal goals to help your brain consider alternatives and possible consequences before going with your first impulse. When your brain wants the "now" option, it's seeking immediate pleasure instead of working toward a goal. A scan of your brain would reveal more activity in your emotional networks. If you choose to postpone immediate pleasure to achieve a goal, your brain activity is greater in the higher prefrontal cortex networks of executive functions. Making these choices gave you the power to override your "now" emotional reactions to achieve your goal of greater reward by resisting the immediate lower payment.

With the experiences you just had, your brain is primed for building your ability to resist jumping to conclusions and taking risks without considering the consequences, and to forego immediate pleasure to achieve a bigger long-term goal.

Sparking Your Synapses

Go back to the list of outcome goals you chose. Select one or two things from the list that could come up in the next week. Write them down with space next to each. ▱

As you build your skills using the brain boosters in the next key, return to this list and write down the strategies you plan to use to resist impulsive first choices and make wiser decisions. For example, if a goal is to stop sending texts or putting postings on Facebook that you later regret, you could select a strategy that has you wait a designated time after writing but before posting.

As you build your impulse-control skills, they'll eventually become automatic routines that help you reach your goals. You can return to the list of goals you write today and enjoy the brain boost of seeing the list get smaller as you achieve more of the goals.

What Boosted Your Brainpower?

You can use these questions as guides for your self-evaluation, or choose your own reflection questions. ▱

- What did I do that was the best use of my time?
- What improvement did I first notice?

- What did I try that I'd do again?
- What would I do differently next time?
- What other strategy from this key do I think will boost my brainpower?

You can create a chart like this one to help you in your evaluation.

Date	Strategy I Tried	What I Noticed
Day 1		
Day 2		
Day 3		
Day 4		
Day 5		

Key 14

Resisting First Responses

*As you learn to weigh the consequences of your
choices and resist the pull of high-risk behaviors,
you'll be not only safer but also smarter.*

WIIFY?

- Avoiding posting or sending texts that you might later
  regret
- Resisting the strong pull to play a game or chat with
  friends when you know you have to do work
- Saving yourself from serious or even fatal injury
- Thinking before buying something you don't really want
  or can't afford
- Preventing yourself from saying things in anger that
  you'll soon regret

Gray Matter

You are more likely to die during your teens than at any other
future time until you are elderly; the teen death rate from pre-
ventable causes is three times that of any other stage of life.

Here's the problem. As a teen, you're growing into an adult body and have access to the same risky temptations as adults do—for example, alcohol, drugs, and driving while texting. However, your teen brain is far from its adult neural maturation. During these years, as your body reaches peaks of surging hormones, strength, coordination, and endurance, you're in a danger zone. It's not because you're bad or thoughtless, but because you don't yet have the strongly wired executive functions of judgment, risk-resistance, and considered decision making that enable you to resist the temptation of instant gratification or to heed the warnings about risky behaviors, even though you have the information and reasoning to understand the potential for harm. These moderating functions are needed to resist the pull of potential dopamine pleasure your brain anticipates arising from risky actions and to make thoughtful choices after first considering potential negative outcomes.

Setting the Stage for Success

Power up the message to your brain by writing a few words about times when you've already resisted your first response and made a more thoughtful choice. ☞ These examples from other teens may help you remember your own.

- I resisted peer pressure and didn't laugh when friends were making fun of another student.
- I tried a little longer to work out a math problem before looking up the answer online or in the answer key.
- I finished my book report and was ready to never see it again, but then I realized there were probably some mistakes in spelling or grammar that I could fix if I read it over, so I did.
- I wanted to eat that third piece of pizza, but I realized I was pretty full, so even though it would taste great, I decided not to eat it.
- I was doing great on a video game and was ready to go to the next level, but I saw it was really late and made myself go to bed so that I wouldn't be wiped out in school the next day.

- I knew I could probably get away lying to my parents so I could go to a party they didn't want me to be at, but I decided to be up front about it and ask their permission.

Thinking about how resisting your first responses can move you closer to your goals will also boost your impulse self-management. Here's what other teens said they wanted to achieve (and did):

- Stop keeping my phone on all night for text and email alerts so that I can sleep better and not write responses when I'm half asleep that I regret in the morning
- Trust myself and not my friends when they "dare" me to do something I don't think is safe
- Avoid getting caught in embarrassing lies because I've made up things to impress the people I'm with.
- Stop posting so many personal photos on my Facebook page and stop posting as many embarrassing selfies on all those websites.

Brain Boosters

Since you usually know what the smart choice is, it's not a lack of knowledge that results in risk taking or decisions you regret; it's your brain programming for pleasure seeking. You can overpower this programming through strategies that build your mental resistance.

In situations like the ones below, the most thoughtful decision is pretty clear. However, by thinking out *how* you'd explain (to a younger relative or to an imaginary younger "you") your reasons for the obvious choices you'd make, you'll build a mental plan or system of analysis that you can apply to other situations.

- Why wouldn't you let a child drive a car?
- Why wouldn't you eat any mushroom you find in the woods?
- Why wouldn't you let your dog loose to roam around alone in a new neighborhood?

Boosting your dopamine in advance of a situation where you might be faced with risky choices (for example, before a party where there will be drugs or alcohol) is another helpful strategy. Your naturally boosted dopamine can be a shield to reduce your brain's hunger for that high-risk pleasure. Try activities like these:

- Listening to music
- Doing some enjoyable physical activity
- Remembering something very pleasurable in your past or something you are really looking forward to in the coming week
- Watching a funny video
- Playing a video game you enjoy with players you like

Sparking Your Synapses

By considering the possible outcomes of your choices, both benefits and risks, you'll be more confident when you do decide that your first response is indeed a good one, and you'll have the willpower to override your brain's impulsive drives when you choose to.

As you read through the strategies to build resistance and take control of the choices you make, write down the ones that you think could be useful for you. 🖎

- When you solve problems in math or science, take the time to find another way to get the same solution. You'll be opening your brain to the reality of more than the first response or choice that comes to mind.
- When you come up with an idea for an art project you're designing or a report you're planning, consider one more way of doing it. Then evaluate which of the two will have the best outcome.
- When you're reading a novel or a history book that presents resolutions to problems or historical disputes, stop and consider what might have resulted in a better outcome.
- When you're reading email, Facebook postings, blogs, or books that demonstrate negative consequences resulting

from other people's bad choices, think about what might
have been a better decision for them to make.

- Before posting on your social media or responding to a
text about something personal or private, wait several
minutes. Take that time to consider any possible negative consequences that could result from an impulsive
post or text.
- When you have an important decision to make, even if
you are pretty sure, take a full minute to think if there
could be potential bad results from the choice.

From the list of strategies you jotted down, put a check next to
any you think you might find useful in the next week or so.

What Boosted Your Brainpower?

You can use these questions as guides for your self-evaluation,
or choose your own reflection questions.

- What did I do that was the best use of my time?
- What improvement did I first notice?
- What did I try that I'd do again?
- What would I do differently next time?
- What other strategy from this key do I think will boost my
brainpower?

You can create a chart like this one to help you in your
evaluation.

Date	Strategy I Tried	What I Noticed
Day 1		
Day 2		
Day 3		
Day 4		
Day 5		

Key 15

Activating Your Powers to Push Boundaries

Now is the prime time for you to explore, while your brain is open to follow dreams even when the outcomes seem impossible.

WIIFY?

- Discovering something no one else ever saw
- Uncovering skills, talents, and interests you didn't know you had
- Exploring new friendship groups and finding amazing people you love spending time with
- Using your curiosity to power your successful learning and expand your skills

Gray Matter

Levels of the reward-response neurochemical dopamine are at an all-time high during the teen years, and greater numbers of dopamine receptors further enhance the pleasure response when dopamine is released.

Although you might need to build executive-function skills to resist your dopamine-driven pleasure seeking, this enhanced pleasure response also has a positive side—your unique teen brain superpowers that motivate exploration and pushing limits are at their peak. Tapping into your brain's flexibility allows you to be open to new experiences and opportunities as they arise.

Setting the Stage for Success

Although so much of this book is about boosting your executive functions, it would be unfortunate if your functions of self-control and following only known pathways were so fully developed that you always made the same old choices because they had worked before. Think of what you'd have missed if you were tied down to ordering only vanilla ice cream because it was the first flavor you ever tried; you liked it and didn't chance exploring other flavors.

Before your brain transitions into an adult brain, more resistant to trying new things and exploring new pathways, think back to times when you did explore beyond a single something that worked out, and so expanded your world.

Look at this list of variations, options, alternatives, and experiences that may have already enriched your life because you tapped into your brain's ability to explore. Write down any examples that bring to mind times when you tried different options or took creative risks with positive outcomes.

- Tried a different way than the instructions indicated to build something or use something
- Instead of following your parents' ways of looking at the world or doing things, came up with a different point of view or approach
- Resisted following the usual rule, pathway, or procedure and discovered a better one for you
- Created new games and cool imaginary worlds with friends
- Tried a new sport and found you liked it
- Went to a movie you didn't expect to like, and discovered a director or actor who led you to more great movies

- Created something in art that gave you pleasure
- Took the chance of spending time with or asking out someone new, and ended up with a great new friend

Brain Boosters

In our rapidly changing world, employers seek resourceful problem solvers, flexible thinkers, and innovators. They want to hire people who are responsive to change and are able to generate original ideas from new information and technology. Enjoy your brain's exploratory drives and you'll also be building creative brainpowers that will serve you well in your future career.

- When trying to solve a problem, try different ways beyond the first one that works or the same solution others have done.
- When you are curious about something, or skeptical about something said to be true, use that feeling to drive your investigation and see where it leads you.
- Observe others for things they are passionate about to discover possible new interests, hobbies, and directions that might be great for you.
- Even when your days are filled with your current sports, clubs, and community activities, invest the time to give new ones a try, because this is a time in your life when you'll be amazed at the things you didn't know about.
- Explore new friendship groups and discover amazing lifelong friendships you might never have begun without pushing your boundaries.
- Set goals you want to achieve and take on new challenges to try, even if success is not guaranteed.

Sparking Your Synapses

Henry Ford, founder of the Ford Motor Company, once said, "Whether you think you can, or whether you think you can't, either way, you are usually right." Don't believe others who tell you that things are impossible or that you don't have what it takes. Take creative risks and make mistakes now so that you become an adult who perceives problems as opportunities, creates positive change, and innovates beyond the status quo. You'll be surprised at what you can do.

To start you off with your brainpower ignited, write down some things that you think might be exciting, fun, enjoyable, or fulfilling that you don't already do. Don't put the brakes on any idea because of nagging negatives, like doubts about your ability, finances, location, intelligence, or skills.

The goal here is to preheat your brain to look for new avenues to explore so that it will be on the alert for possible opportunities as you go about your day. Without the baggage of "I don't think I can" holding back your brain's adventurousness, you'll be primed to recognize things you want to do, people you want to meet, and pathways you want to explore.

These suggestions can help you get started:

- Spend time with people who are passionate about what they do and see if their enthusiasm sparks your interest in their hobby, club, sport, or job.
- Look at the listing of your community recreation department, where you'll find a variety of sports, clubs, art class, clubs, and other activities. You don't even have to commit to joining, but a great start is to observe a session and let your interest and curiosity guide your explorations.
- Go through the catalogue or online course listings for your local community college—a great source of ideas to explore. These classes can be very hands on and not like the classes you sit in all day. You'll find art, computer, animation, cooking, hiking, sports—and don't forget bow and arrow making. Most schools allow you to sit in the first class to see if you like it. You may discover a whole new interest and group of people!

Write down your possibilities, select one or two that really stand out, and make some notes about what you'll look for or whom you'll seek out to help you explore that dream. 🏹

The list you make powers up your brain's interest and effort. You now have the brainpower to recognize and light up pathways to explore that will not be as open once you take on the focuses of careers and family. You don't have to follow every dream but do allow yourself to dream and see where they might lead.

What Boosted Your Brainpower?

You can use these questions as guides for your self-evaluation, or choose your own reflection questions.

- What did I do that was the best use of my time?
- What improvement did I first notice?
- What did I try that I'd do again?
- What would I do differently next time?
- What other strategy from this key do I think will boost my brainpower?

You can create a chart like this one to help you in your evaluation.

Date	Strategy I Tried	What I Noticed
Day 1		
Day 2		
Day 3		
Day 4		
Day 5		

Key 16
Making Good Mistakes

*Mistakes help your brain build stronger memories
so that you can meet future challenges.*

WIIFY?

- Expanding your boundaries by risking smart mistakes
- Turning mistakes into guidance systems for success
- Conquering the fear of making mistakes in front of classmates

Gray Matter

Sure, you are able to learn things when you do drill on something over and over. But you're missing out on forging the strongest possible memories (as well as discoveries) if you don't tap into your dopamine reward system's mistake response. When you take the risk of trying, you not only build a stronger understanding but also hook into the unique chemistry of your teen brain, to make faster, stronger memories in response to making mistakes.

With your dopamine response levels at their peak, your brain is driven to get the pleasure that comes from achieving challenges, including solving problems and figuring out the answers to questions. When you make a prediction (try out a solution) that doesn't work, your brain experiences a bit of frustration because it didn't get its dopamine. This slight setback drives your brain to change itself so that it will get the dopamine reward triggered by a successful choice the next time.

That the brain would learn from mistakes makes sense for survival. When you make a mistake and then take the time to think about a better choice or answer, your brain takes this correct information and wires it into the faulty memory network to replace the misinformation. That's why the strongest understandings you have, which guide your best future answers and choices, don't come from what you memorized but rather from what you learn from failure.

Setting the Stage for Success

If you never tried challenges and suffered mistakes and failures, your brain would not know about what brings pleasure or unpleasantness. Your parents may have told you as a small child not to put soap in your mouth, but if you were like most little kids, their instructions weren't enough for you to really learn that information. When you did taste soap, it tasted horrible. It was trying it yourself and finding out it was a mistake that built the understanding and wired the memory that kept you from eating soap again. So you've already learned from and succeeded from your mistakes—unless you still eat soap.

Making mistakes has already expanded your world and your knowledge. When you made and corrected an error on a math test or put together an outfit that didn't work but gave you ideas for a better one, your brain built new wiring that subsequently guided you to a better choice the next time and thereafter. Take an inventory of mistakes from which you've learned:

- Making a wrong turn when walking, hiking, or driving and discovering something cool you didn't know was there

- Mistakes you made on a quiz that encouraged you to go back and review that topic so that you got the questions about it right on the big test
- Picking up the wrong color and using it in a painting or the wrong ingredient and using it in a recipe, and discovering you liked it—or because of an outcome you didn't like, becoming more attentive to checking your ingredients or colors

You'll get even more material for your inventory by asking your parents about mistakes you made and learned from as a young child. Then ask them about some of their whopper mistakes that will make you laugh—and learn.

Brain Boosters

Strategies exist to help you learn from your mistakes and turn them into greater wisdom. Remember that for the simple price of trying, making mistakes, and letting your brain then wire in the right information, you'll build a real understanding and memories that last.

Jot down a few that you'll try out. 🗒

- Before asking someone how to solve a problem, try it yourself. In one research study, students who tried, even unsuccessfully, to solve a type of math problem were ultimately the best at learning and remembering when they were later given an applicable strategy.
- Even if you feel discouraged by mistakes you see you've made when a test is returned, take the opportunity to find out the right answers so that your eager brain will wire in the correct information for future use.
- Ask teachers or students who took the class before what common misunderstandings or mistakes have been made involving the topic you are starting. You'll be more attentive to that information and know what pitfalls to avoid.

- If you frequently make the same type of mistake on certain types of tests or assignments, keep a list of the type of mistakes you make and want to avoid.
- Before starting a test or assignment on which you are prone to making the same type of mistakes, write a few words (on scrap paper) to remind you of the mistakes to avoid; for example, *estimate to see if my answer is reasonable* or *read my writing quietly aloud to find errors before turning it in.*
- Keep an ongoing list of mistakes that you learn from starting today. When you're down on yourself about new mistakes, review that list of mistakes that made you smarter.

Sparking Your Synapses

Basketball star Michael Jordan said, "I've missed more than 9,000 shots in my career. I've lost almost 300 games. I've failed over and over and over again in my life. And that is why I succeed."

Instead of deciding your mistakes are signs of failure, maximize your brain's mistake response to increase your future success. Write something you will try this week, such as answering a question in class, where it is possible you'll make a mistake. Use the inspiration from Michael Jordan's quotation to spark your synapses into following through on that action.

What Boosted Your Brainpower?

You can use these questions as guides for your self-evaluation, or choose your own reflection questions.

- What did I do that was the best use of my time?
- What improvement did I first notice?
- What did I try that I'd do again?
- What would I do differently next time?
- What other strategy from this key do I think will boost my brainpower?

You can create a chart like this one to help you in your evaluation.

Date	Strategy I Tried	What I Noticed
Day 1		
Day 2		
Day 3		
Day 4		
Day 5		

DOOR FIVE

MEMORY

Wiring in new memories is a matter of linking the new with the known. Making strong memories quickly and keeping the memories you construct from fading away after a test or over the summer is one of the biggest time savers and brainpower conservers there is. As you learn to remember what you hear, learn, read, practice, and review, you'll build strong and efficient memory networks—strong enough to last over time so that you won't have to relearn everything again and again.

Key 17

Taking Control of What Sticks in Your Memory

*You can tap into the unique memory speed your brain
has as a result of its awesome transitions
at this stage of your life.*

WIIFY?

- Understanding and remembering more of what you hear in class and do for homework
- Remembering things you need to do
- Retaining necessary information people tell you
- Recalling what you studied when you take a test
- Remembering what you studied *even after the test ends*

Gray Matter

Every year, there is more to memorize. Using neuroscience research about memory, you can select strategies that can help you remember what you hear, learn, and read—even through the summer, avoiding the need to relearn everything again.

Beginning at age twelve and continuing for the next decade, the human brain boosts its learning power and memory construction. The reason for this boost is the supercharged construction speed of your brain's neuroplasticity as it transitions through the teen years. At no other time in your life will your memory circuits be wired stronger, requiring a smaller number of reinforcing repetitions (activations of the synapses where memories are constructed).

Basically, your brain is a pattern-seeking organ. It is always on the alert and absorbs characteristics of new information that might be similar to the patterns of related ideas and knowledge stored in your existing memory circuits. You understand and remember what is novel through this wonderful brain programming, which holds on to new information by linking it to related information previously stored in your memory banks.

Setting the Stage for Success

Take a moment to recognize examples of the superpowered learning and memory speed that you've experienced in the past several years. Some examples of your brain's rapid construction of skill or information memory might be the speed at which you picked up a sports skill (for example, snowboarding, mountain biking, boogie boarding, volleyball, or skimboarding), a musical instrument, the rules of a new game or sport, words to a song, or even a new language that came to you if you moved to or spent time in another country.

Write down a few examples of things you learned in a fairly short time—faster than younger siblings and especially your parents. Recognizing how you can learn and remember more in less time can fuel your effort expended for the increased memorizing challenges you now face. 🗒

Brain Boosters

As you learn how to activate the memories you already have to hook on to and hold new learning, you'll superpower your memory-building success.

To boost your patterning power, it helps to experience it. Below are opportunities to develop awareness of how your brain knows to make sense of new things. First, read the paragraph below to see how your brain responds to unfamiliar information by relating it to similar patterns already stored in your memory.

Cna yuo raed tihs? You can uesdnatnrd waht you are rdanieg bcuse of patrning. It dseno't mtaetr in waht oerdr the ltteres in a wrod are, the iproamtnt tihng is taht the frsit and lsat ltteer be in the rghit pclae. The rset can be a taotl mses, and you can sitll raed it whotuit a pboerlm. Tihs is bcuseae the huamn mnid deos not raed ervey lteter by istlef, but the words aer rcognisd as patrns.

What happened? Although you'd never seen most of the words before, you are an experienced reader. Your brain used the patterns that it built up when you learned to read to figure out the words that were not spelled correctly. There were enough familiar word patterns in the mixed-up words for your brain to use its memory of stored words to "translate" the new words into known words. Pretty neat, huh?

You can further boost your brain's buy-in to using patterning power by recalling things you learned and stored in related memory circuits that you've frequently used to figure out, understand, predict, or evaluate new experiences or questions. Write down ones that you've experienced and even one or two more you can think of that are not listed. When you write these down, take a moment to recognize how you tapped into your brain's pattern seeking and recognition to make the new connection. ⎙

- Estimating the number of items in a jar
- Using memories of words signaling the process called for to know if a math word problem wanted you to add or subtract (for example, *How many less than, What was the sum, How many were left over,* or *All together how many*)
- In a new place, figuring out north, south, east, west based on the sun's position
- Predicting what food might be cooking based on the smells that reached you

- Remembering facts that you learned in the rhymes or songs you sang or heard repeatedly (for example, "The Alphabet Song" or "Fifty Nifty States")
- Preparing a dish you've often made without having to look up the recipe
- Shopping for snacks without having to add up their cost to be sure your $10 would cover them.
- Filling your gas tank without reading the instructions on the pump after doing it a few times

Any others?

Sparking Your Synapses

Now that you've experienced your brain's patterning system as key to memory construction, you can tap into that system to get new memory to stick by linking the new to the known in your short-term memory, which is the first stage in building long-term memory.

Creating analogies is a most powerful strategy for this linking. After reading the two sample analogies here, write your own for any two words you need to learn for school this week. These could be vocabulary words (in English or your foreign language), new terminology in math or science, or events in history. You'll see how powerful your brain's patterning is as new memory glue. ☐

Word: *Dopamine*
Analogy: *Dopamine* is to pleasure what sugar is to sweetness.

Word: *Neuroplasticity*
Analogy: *Neuroplasticity* builds brainpower like exercise builds muscle.

What Boosted Your Brainpower?

You can use these questions as guides for your self-evaluation, or choose your own reflection questions. ☐

- What did I do that was the best use of my time?
- What improvement did I first notice?
- What did I try that I'd do again?
- What would I do differently next time?
- What other strategy from this key do I think will boost my brainpower?

You can create a chart like this one to help you in your evaluation.

Date	Strategy I Tried	What I Noticed
Day 1		
Day 2		
Day 3		
Day 4		
Day 5		

Key 18

Depositing Memories for Easy Withdrawal

Start building your multisensory memory habits now, and you'll free up time simply by studying for tests faster and more effectively.

WIIFY?

- Discovering how to boost your memory power by using more of your senses
- Experiencing much easier recall of what you need to remember
- Choosing how you want to study things you need to remember (and enjoying less stress and more success as a result)
- Building strong memory circuits that last test after test, year after year

Gray Matter

Often, more than one of something comes in handy; for example, when you're looking for a pen, need an ATM, or are seeking a gas station in your town, especially when there are road closures

117

or you don't know exactly where you are. The same benefit applies when you store multiple deposits of memories throughout your brain. It could be that your access to one memory bank is blocked; that is, you can't remember or open that first memory circuit. If you have the information you need to remember stored in different memory banks, it's much easier to find one you can withdraw from when you need it.

The reason you can deposit memory in multiple brain banks is because your brain stores memory in different regions that correspond to each of your senses. Memory of things you *hear* are stored in the regions on the sides of your brain (your temporal lobes), those you *see* in the back of the brain (occipital lobes), and likewise for different locations that store memories of experiences related to *movement, smell, taste,* or *touch.*

These different sensory memories, stored throughout the brain and related to the same information, link up and connect to each other when they are formed. When needed, remembering just a single way you learned or reviewed the information activates the related information experienced and stored by your other senses.

Here's how it could work for you now. If your science teacher played recordings of sound waves that were matched to visual displays, your brain would store the information in both your visual and sound memory centers. If you add feeling the vibrations from a sound amplifier in your car or at home to those sensory memories, you'll enhance storage of the touch memory in yet another memory vault. When you need to remember any of the information about sound waves, just remembering any one of those experiences activates the others. It doesn't matter which one comes to mind when you are trying to remember facts about sound waves for a test. Recalling the buzzing sensation of the amplifier triggers those other sensory information storehouses to pop into your recall.

Setting the Stage for Success

Do you remember a special day or an emotionally powerful experience? Your last birthday, a big surprise, your first kiss, the day you got your driver's license, a great moment when playing your sport, winning a prize, or getting an award? Think about that time and recall what else you remember about it. See if you can answer any of these questions:

- Who was there with you?
- Where were you?
- What did you eat or drink?
- What was said?
- What objects did you see?
- What else do you remember about that day or special moment?

What you experienced as you discovered your memory of surprising details was the power of multisensory memory. You'll be able to harness that strong memory construction when you use the multisensory memory strategies that follow.

Set the stage for boosting your brainpower by writing a few words about goals you want to achieve by increasing your memory capacity. Even though the strategies are easy, and often enjoyable, it always helps to boost your brain's awareness of the positive outcomes you are working for. 📝

Brain Boosters

Here are some examples of enhanced sensory awareness to increase your memory-building speed and your power to remember what you need. Read the examples in each sensory category. As you complete each list, write down an idea it gives you to boost that sensory intake for something you might study. 📝

Visual

- Visualize the information in a bizarre or funny way, such as animals reenacting a historical event.
- Draw sketches representing the important information in a lecture. (Drawing a sketch of information you hear adds sensory input from both your visual representation and the physical movement of drawing.)

- Use three different colored pens for taking notes, matching the color to importance of the information. For example, you could use green for basic interest, orange for greater importance, and red for critical value.
- Visualize an electron orbiting the nucleus of an atom and make that visualization multisensory by making a buzzing sound like electricity as it whizzes by. (Add another sense by rubbing a balloon on the wall, then holding it above your arm hair to feel the tingle of the static electric charge.)

Smell and Taste

- Associating characters in history or literature with a good or bad smell and/or taste, depending on your opinion of them.
- Smell coffee when studying the exports of Columbia.
- Inhale the curries of India.

Hearing

- While listening to a lecture, pick out the key words and whisper these quietly to yourself so that you create a memory of the sound of your voice and movements of your lips, in addition to your teacher's voice and movements.
- Read textbooks aloud to add auditory data to the visual memory of the words.
- What song comes to mind that you can relate to the lesson information? Can you substitute some of the lesson words into that song as you sing it to yourself?
- Dictate your written notes into phone or computer. Listen to your dictation as you review for the additional auditory sensory memory.

Touch

- Imagine what something you are learning about might feel like if you could touch it. What would the surface of Jupiter feel like? Hot? Cold? Firm? Soft? Powerful?

- Touch something on your desk, in your binder, or in your pocket that you can mentally connect to the information you are learning. For example, for the concept of supply and demand in economics, touch your hungry stomach, then your pocket or wallet as you imagine how much you'd be willing to pay if the top cafeteria choices were very limited in supply and the most expensive.
- With a diagram showing labeled parts, touch each part as you also say its name.

Movement

- Move balls of different sizes around a beach ball "sun" to re-create planetary movement. Even further, walk (re-volve) around the sun ball while turning (rotating) your body counterclockwise—except for Venus, the one planet that spins clockwise on its axis.
- Stand up while reading an important paragraph you want to remember from history or current events and to bring it back to mind, think of the topic as something you "took a stand on" or "stood up for."

Sparking Your Synapses

While doing homework, use more than one sensory system to review or practice. You'll be banking memory storage deposits in multiple vaults for faster access when you need it.

Select something you are now learning (and will need to lock into memory). Write down the name of the fact, rule, or procedure. Next to it write a few words about how you'll secure the information into additional brain storage by experiencing it through another of your senses. ▱

In the very unlikely event that you are fortunate enough not to have anything you need to memorize for school, here are some things for which other teens have used multisensory learning for expanded memory deposits.

- The definition of "medieval"
- Association property of addition
- Foreshadowing as a literary technique
- The precipitation cycle (evaporation, condensation, precipitation)
- Spelling rule of "I before E except after C"
- The causes and events of the Boston Tea Party
- Three types of rocks (igneous, sedentary, metamorphic)

What Boosted Your Brainpower?

You can use these questions as guides for your self-evaluation, or choose your own reflection questions.

- What did I do that was the best use of my time?
- What improvement did I first notice?
- What did I try that I'd do again?
- What would I do differently next time?
- What other strategy from this key do I think will boost my brainpower?

You can create a chart like this one to help you in your evaluation.

Date	Strategy I Tried	What I Noticed
Day 1		
Day 2		
Day 3		
Day 4		
Day 5		

Key 19

Remembering What You Read

*Break the zoned-out habit of reading to the bottom
of a page and realizing that your eyes went over the
words but no information got into your brain.*

WIIFY?

- Understanding more of what you read
- Reading and remembering more in less time
- Boosting dopamine and making the time you have to spend reading boring or really hard books more enjoyable
- Cutting down the amount of rereading or review you need to do when it's test time

Gray Matter

You've no doubt read a page of text, only to get to the bottom and realize you had no clue about what you read. Simply repeating the motions of moving your eyes from one word to the next is likely to result in the same frustration of getting to the end of the page without knowing more than you did when you started.

The problem is with your attention filter. As you read, it seeks out novelty, change, and things that you associate with pleasure. Rereading the same information, if it's personally uninteresting and unchanged between your first reading and the second, will not trigger your attention. If it doesn't make it through your attention filter, it certainly won't become memory. If you link learning to dopamine pleasure, you'll be more successful at remembering what you read.

Setting the Stage for Success

Before taking on some of the strategies outside of this book, boost your brain's expectation of success by exploring your power to discover the meaning of new words without a dictionary.

Your brain picks up the hints from what are called "context clues" when you read. You've experienced how it uses context clues whenever you've read to the end of a sentence and then figured out what an unfamiliar word meant. You do this because you get meaning (context) from the whole sentence that then activates the prior knowledge you have to correctly predict the meaning of the unknown word.

Here's an example. If you don't already know the meaning of the word *temerity*, see if you can predict its meaning after reading these sentences written for vocabulary homework by other teens.

- *No one could believe her temerity when she stole the answer key to the test.*
- *I was amazed at Jake's temerity when he told the teacher that the assignments were unfair and a waste of time.*
- *His older sister was in awe of Caleb when he had the temerity to tell the baby sitter they hated the dinners she made them.*
- *We didn't think he really would do it, but Simon had the temerity to put up a post asking his Facebook friends to send him answers he could use for his homework essay.*
- *Max had the temerity to not only steal Jennifer's lunch, but also to eat it right at her table.*

Now, think of a word or words that could fit in place of "temerity" in some of the sentences. Try it out. If you read the sentences using your definition of "temerity," do they still make sense? Do they make even more sense?

By the way, temerity can mean recklessness, overconfidence, foolhardiness, bad risk-taking, and many more synonyms.

Brain Boosters

Talking back to the text via sticky notes is an interactive reading strategy to help you understand and remember what you read. What's more, you'll have those notes stuck to the textbook to augment your test review, which is especially useful when it is a schoolbook you cannot write notes in.

It is often helpful to select one or more from each category depending on what you are reading. Read through the suggested sticky notes, go back through the list, and write down ones you might want to use. You might find it helpful to group separate lists of stickies best for different types of reading, such as literature, history, and science books.

There are three categories of suggested questions:

- *Before reading*: Most of these are general questions that invite your predictions about what you might read. When you write down your prediction, your brain invests in wanting to know if it has won the "bet" by predicting correctly. To get the prediction triggered dopamine motivation from your brain, fill these out just before you start reading.

  I think you'll be telling me . . .
  I already know things about you, so I predict . . .

- *Preview questions*: These are another type of prediction. They will have the power of brain interest because you "predicted" that you'd find the information to answer them as you did the reading. Again, your brain will be primed and alert to remember the answer to these questions you created because you set it up to want to look for that information. You'll write these after briefly skimming the pages you'll be reading.

> How did this character make the decision to . . .
> Why did they go on the exploration to . . .
> The heading for this section now makes sense because I found out about . . .

- *During reading*: You'll respond to these questions or sentence starters while you're actually reading.

> You are similar to what I have learned before, because you remind me of . . .
> I would have preferred a picture of . . . (Here, you can also sketch or download a picture on your own.)
> I didn't know that, and I find it interesting because . . .
> I disagree because . . .
> This is not what I expected, which was . . .
> This gives me an idea for . . .
> I want to know more about this than you have to offer. I'll find out by . . .
> I have a different way of interpreting this information, which is . . .
> I won't let you get away with this statement, so I'll check your source by . . .
> I think this will be on the test because . . .
> I can put the main ideas of this part of the chapter into a list of ten words, which are . . .

Now try it. Select a reading assignment and copy three or more of these statements onto sticky notes. Before or during your reading, complete the sentences and put the notes into the book. Give yourself an added memory boost by placing blank stickies in your book when there is anything else you read of note that you want to remember.

Highlighting complex text is another great way to understand difficult reading without having to get help or even look up words. For this, you'll need to make a copy or printout of the reading that you can write on. You'll also need highlighters in three different colors. Try this out first on a single page of text. With practice, you'll be able to use it on any text you can mark up.

1. Use the first color (for example, yellow) to highlight the words or phrases you *understand* during the first reading.
2. Then immediately pick up the second color (let's say, blue), without doing anything else, such as looking up vocabulary words or digging through your notes. Read the same page again and highlight anything new you understand. You don't need to highlight full sentences, just phrases and even words will do.
3. As you no doubt predicted, go right to the third reading and use the third color (for example, green) to highlight.

By highlighting, you tickled your attention filter's interest and turned what your brain expected to be a boring reading task into an opportunity for dopamine bursts. You also kept your amygdala from getting into the frustrated stress state of being discouraged from time spent reading without understanding.

It's likely you used context clues earlier to come up with synonyms for temerity. In the same way, when you reread something in the way described in these brainpower boosters, when you won't be too stressed out to keep your mind on it, you will use the information you do understand to fill in meaning for the parts that you don't "get" the first time.

Sparking Your Synapses

Power up the message to your brain by selecting two reading assignments you need to do this week. Include one that you dread because it's time-consuming or boring and another that's a challenge to understand, such as one with difficult vocabulary or science words. Write down which boring assignment you'll try out with the sticky notes and which hard one you'll pick to try out the highlighting. Then write a few words about what you'll get from using the strategy. For example, "By writing, 'You are similar to what I have learned before, because you remind me of . . . ,' I'll be preheating memories I already have. These will become hooks that hold on to the new information I need to remember from the reading."

For the highlighting, you might predict a positive outcome such as, "It will boost my brainpower to see more and more highlighting with each of the readings and colors. Instead of high-lighted sections showing me what I don't know and what I have to study, these highlighted sections will show me my progress— what I figured out and know."

Make your own list of a few things you'll enjoy when you can memorize what you need in less time and remember it much longer.

What Boosted Your Brainpower?

You can use these questions as guides for your self-evaluation, or choose your own reflection questions.

- What did I do that was the best use of my time?
- What improvement did I first notice?
- What did I try that I'd do again?
- What would I do differently next time?
- What other strategy from this key do I think will boost my brainpower?

You can create a chart like this one to help you in your evaluation.

Date	Strategy I Tried	What I Noticed
Day 1		
Day 2		
Day 3		
Day 4		
Day 5		

Key 20

Building Memories That Last

*Transform fragile new learning into
solidly wired long-term memory.*

WIIFY?

- Discovering methods of review and studying to make the strongest memories
- Studying more efficiently
- Using study strategies that are more enjoyable than drilling over and over
- Tweeting your way to test success

Gray Matter

When your brain first links the new with the known in short-term memory, the connections are few and weak. But every time you activate a memory (for example, by writing down a phone number you just heard), an electrical current travels from one neuron to the next in the circuit, with each holding a small part of the memory. That electrical current triggers the neuroplastic response so more connections sprout. This allows both more efficient communication from neuron to neuron, and thicker insulation (myelin) is laid down around the connections. There seems to be no limit in terms of the strength or amount of information you can hold in the neural networks you construct through neuroplasticity.

Not all types of study or review activate short-term memories equally. Those that involve doing something active with those memories (rather than rote memorization) are the most effective at using your neuroplasticity to construct strong, fast, durable, memory banks ready for solving problems, innovating creatively, and applying to goals beyond a single test or classroom session.

Setting the Stage for Success

Listening to stories was probably one of the most powerful and pleasurable patterns your brain constructed during childhood. First of all, being told or read a story by someone who cared about you, it was highly likely that you were in a good emotional place. For someone to read you a story meant that things were pretty calm. Often you were cozy, snuggled in your bed.

While the stories of your childhood are linked in your memory with positive emotional experiences, they also produced a mental map for remembering events in a sequence. Your brain is greatly attracted to the familiar, comforting pattern of all the stories you loved. This is the four-step progression:

1. Beginning (*Once upon a time . . .*)
2. Problem
3. Resolution
4. Ending (*. . . and they all lived happily ever after.*)

You can take a challenging description of the circulatory system or a boring unit from history class and transform the information you are required to learn into something very brain-friendly by using the memorable pattern of those childhood stories.

By transforming learning into a story, it becomes not only more interesting, but with your brain engaged, dopamine ignited, and very familiar patterns activated, you'll remember the information with a surprising ease and staying power.

Here's an example:

Beginning: *Once upon a time* the colonists living in what is now the United States were under the rule of the king who ruled Great Britain.

Problem: The British were making the colonists pay high taxes on things they needed and not allowing them to have any say in the laws they had to follow.

Resolution: The colonists protested and eventually fought a war that forced the British to give them independence.

Ending: The struggle for independence was victorious for the colonists and ended with the birth of a new nation. We celebrate that momentous achievement each year on the Fourth of July.

Select a lesson, unit, or chapter from any subject that you don't yet have set in memory but need to know. As you review the information, jot down a few notes putting the information in story pattern. It doesn't have to be a detailed story, or even have complete sentences.

Beyond turning new learning into a story, you could also transform it into a skit, a dance, a song, or a poem. You could create a webpage, a video, or write a news story or fictionalized interview. Experience the motivation of choosing your own creative fuel!

Brain Boosters

Teaching someone else is yet another way to transform information. You'll be impressed by how much effort your brain puts forth when you face the challenge of teaching information to someone younger or without any knowledge about the topic.

Information is truly hard wired in your memory when you can teach it to someone.

The mental manipulation of this booster starts with the dopamine-pleasure expectation of choice: Who will be your audience? It can be a real person or someone you keep in mind while planning and recording yourself giving the lesson or lessons. If you'd like to get feedback in steps so that you can adjust teaching plans, divide the topic into several segments.

After teaching a segment to an actual person, ask your "student" what he or she understood from the information you taught. You'll get the powerful feedback of how well you understand the information based on the understanding the student gets from your lesson.

You can get rich feedback even from your self-recorded lessons just by listening to your segments as you go. You'll recognize the sections you understand best by the smoothness and clarity of your "teaching." You'll have the benefit of being able to go back to your source, boost your understanding, then teach the person or dictate the section again and see the improvement.

Throughout this process, your brain will have clear and reachable goals in mind. You'll be reading or reviewing information actively because you're running it through your brain thinking how to best represent it to someone else. You'll find that your brain will want to go back to the book or notes more frequently than if you were just studying for a test, because it sees the opportunity of rereading and thinking as keys to achieving the challenge it seeks—successful understanding by your student. You'll receive empowering dopamine boosts as you try and succeed or try, revise, and succeed building your memory by reinforcing your student's understanding.

Assignments often require you to summarize the information from a chapter by taking notes about important topics in the unit. These are usually pretty passive ways of connecting with the information. Often students skim the chapter to copy phrases or subtitles and a few facts about each or just copy the bold subheads and the first sentence of each paragraph. Summaries like those hardly help your brain build a strong memory circuit.

But there is a very powerful type of summarizing that really boosts your understanding and memory. Long before Twitter existed, Albert Einstein said, "If you can't explain it simply, you don't understand it well enough." Studies where students who evaluated and discussed the main ideas of a unit presented with tweets did indeed understand and remember more than those who passively read dense pages of descriptive text indeed suggested Einstein was on to something you can use. When you take notes in class or read in your textbook, give your brain the sharp understanding that comes when you define big ideas into the concise summaries of tweets.

The tweets below carry lots of information in their small packages. They show that the writers understood the important message about the relationship of neuroplasticity and memory.

- *Mentally manipulating pumps neuroplasticity—makes durable long-term memory*
- *To learn something new start with something old. Connecting the with the known is memory gold*
- *Neuroplastic brains turn new information into learning that lasts*

Select any chapter you've completed in this workbook and write a tweet about it. You can just write it in your notebook with the 140-character limit (including spaces, punctuation, and numbers) or send it as a text message or an email to yourself.

You might find yourself wanting to go back and to reread parts of the information, even though this is a practice activity and you aren't being graded or tested. That effort to go back to reread or to write more than one version of your tweet stems from your dopamine working. Composing a tweet is an achievable challenge that doesn't take long and gives your brain an almost immediate feedback of satisfaction when you finish one you like. So give it a try and feel your dopamine motivation.

What happened when you summarized your information in a tight little tweet? You can take a moment to self-evaluate your experience or read on now about what others noticed.

- "I really thought hard about what it meant because I couldn't just copy a few sentences."
- "Compressing all the information into the small tweet made my brain really think about what it meant. I definitely understood it more."
- "I got more out of it when I had to compress it into a tweet. The next day in class, I was able to follow the discussions much better than usual."
- "I don't really like history, and when I read and take notes, I just try to get through it as quickly as I can. I never reread anything. When I had to make the tweet, I found myself going back to reread parts and it was actually interesting—which never happens."

From your self-evaluation of your tweet experience or from relating to things that happened to others, write a few notes (or a tweet) about what seemed to happen in your brain when you created your tweet. Did you understand the material better, find yourself going back to the text as you composed your tweet, feel the memory was stronger than usual, and even enjoy the learning experience more than usual? 🗹

Sparking Your Synapses

Select something you need to remember for school and choose a mental manipulation strategy you read about in this key. Jot down a brief description of your plan next to the topic you choose, as in the examples below. Later, return to the page in your notebook to write about how it boosted your understanding and memory. 🗹

- To remember the climate, local agriculture, points of interest, and unique products of the regions in the French countryside, I'll design travel brochures, in French, to entice Parisians to visit other regions of the country.
- To understand and remember what we're learning in science about electric circuits and magnetic fields, I'll design

an electromagnetic engine that increases distances cars can go without a recharge.
- I really like time travel games, like *Assassin's Creed*. I'll use the information I read and hear about in our biology unit about bacteria to plan what I'd take back with me to fourteenth-century Europe to limit the devastation of the plague.

What Boosted Your Brainpower?

You can use these questions as guides for your self-evaluation, or choose your own reflection questions.

- What did I do that was the best use of my time?
- What improvement did I first notice?
- What did I try that I'd do again?
- What would I do differently next time?
- What other strategy from this key do I think will boost my brainpower?

You can create a chart like this one to help you in your evaluation.

Date	Strategy I Tried	What I Noticed
Day 1		
Day 2		
Day 3		
Day 4		
Day 5		

A Closing Note for Teens

Congratulations on caring enough about yourself to read this book, trying some of the strategies, and for the efforts you'll continue to make. You now have the brainpower to recognize and light up pathways to explore that will not be as open once you take on the focuses of careers and family. You don't have to follow every dream but do allow yourself to dream and see where they might lead.

You are the future, and you are on the way to embracing the opportunities that await you in the twenty-first century.

. . . And One for Adults

Your engagement with this book has ideally built your and your teen's understanding about the powerful applications of neuroscience research to building strong executive functions, memory, and goal-achievement success. The impact of your collaboration with your teen has no doubt been increasingly evident as he or she has used neuroplasticity power and guided strategies to become more self-directed, organized, motivated, and successful.

I applaud your efforts in helping your child reduce stress and increasingly enjoy learning, exploring, and connecting with you and others. As a mother, physician, and teacher, I admire you for taking the time to provide the resources of this book—and yourself—to your teen. You've increased your child's access to reaching his or her full potential as a student, citizen, and future guardian of our planet.

Because of your support, encouragement, and the tools you shared, your child's happiness, success, curiosity, resilience, and wisdom will continue to grow through a lifetime of experiences and opportunities.

About the Author

Dr. Judy Willis, a board-certified neurologist, combined her fifteen years as a practicing neurologist with ten subsequent years as a classroom teacher to become a leading authority in the neuroscience of learning. With her unique background both in neuroscience and education, she has written eight books and more than two hundred articles about applying neuroscience research to classroom teaching strategies.

After graduating Phi Beta Kappa as the first woman graduate from Williams College, Willis attended UCLA School of Medicine where she was awarded her medical degree. She remained at UCLA and completed a medical residency and neurology residency, including chief residency. She practiced neurology for fifteen years before returning to university to obtain her teaching credential and master of education degree from the University of California, Santa Barbara. She then taught in elementary and secondary school for ten years.

Dr. Willis now travels nationally and internationally giving presentations, workshops, and consulting about learning and the brain. She is on the adjunct faculty of Williams College and the board of directors of The Hawn Foundation. Dr. Willis has been interviewed by *USA Today*, *Euronews*, *Wall Street Journal*, NBC News's *Education Nation*, ABC Australia Radio, *Lateline Australia*, *Popular Mechanics*, *Neurology Today*, the *Washington*

Post, Education Week, Medscope Neurology, TEDx videos, NPJ *Science of Learning Journal, Scholastic Magazine,* and *Parenting Magazine* among others. She writes staff expert blogs for NBC News *Education Nation, Edutopia, Psychology Today,* and the *Guardian.* In 2011, Dr. Willis was honored by *Edutopia* as a "Big Thinker in Education."

Website: R. A. D. by Judy Willis M.D., M.Ed., www.RADTeach .com.